Dr. Seuss from THEN to NOW

"Mr. Mayor! Mr. Mayor!" Horton called
from *Horton Hears a Who!*, 1954 [113].

Dr. Seuss from THEN to NOW

A Catalogue
of the Retrospective
Exhibition

Organized by the
San Diego Museum of Art
San Diego, California
1986

RANDOM HOUSE NEW YORK

Dr. Seuss from Then to Now is published on the occasion of an exhibition organized by the San Diego Museum of Art and shown at:

San Diego Museum of Art
San Diego, California
17 May–13 July 1986

Cedar Rapids Museum of Art
Cedar Rapids, Iowa
27 September–14 December 1986

Carnegie Museum of Art and the Carnegie Library of Pittsburgh
Pittsburgh, Pennsylvania
10 January–1 March 1987

LTV Center Pavillion
Dallas, Texas
4 April–21 June 1987

Tampa Museum of Art
Tampa, Florida
26 September–8 November 1987

The Baltimore Museum of Art
Baltimore, Maryland
5 December 1987–17 January 1988

New Orleans Museum of Art
New Orleans, Louisiana
13 February–10 April 1988

The national tour and local presentation of *Dr. Seuss from Then to Now* are made possible by gifts from Allied-Signal Inc., the James S. Copley Foundation, Cecil and Ida Green, Ingrid and Joseph Hibben, and Home Federal.

Numbers in brackets refer to entries in the Checklist of the Exhibition.

 Published in the United States by Random House, Inc., New York, and simultaneously in Canada by Random House of Canada Limited, Toronto. Originally published by the San Diego Museum of Art in 1986.

Library of Congress Cataloging-in-Publication Data: Dr. Seuss from then to now. Bibliography: p. 1. Seuss, Dr.—Exhibitions. 2. Illustration of books—20th century—United States—Exhibitions. I. Seuss, Dr. II. San Diego Museum of Art.
NC975.5.S48A4 1987 700′.92′4 87-4838 ISBN: 0-394-89268-2 (hardcover)
Manufactured in the United States of America 1 2 3 4 5 6 7 8 9 0

Contents

THIS BOOK IS FOR
MY DAD
BIG TED of SPRINGFIELD THE FINEST MAN I'LL EVER KNOW

Dedication page, ***If I Ran the Circus,*** 1956 [118].

Acknowledgments

The national tour of the exhibition *Dr. Seuss from Then to Now* would not have been possible without the enthusiastic support of many individuals and institutions. Patrons and staff of the San Diego Museum of Art as well as colleagues, libraries, and other museums throughout the country and, of course, Ted Geisel himself committed countless hours to the many complex aspects of organizing the exhibition and catalogue. The result of these efforts will, we trust, enlighten and entertain thousands of visitors and introduce to all the many wonderful works of Dr. Seuss.

We wish to extend our sincere gratitude to Ted and Audrey Geisel for their support and goodwill despite a curatorial invasion of their home and studio over a five-month period. The insights and invaluable suggestions offered by Mr. Geisel during the research and planning of the exhibition were pivotal to the project's development.

The curator of the exhibition, Mary Stofflet, devoted herself to the project with her usual boundless enthusiasm, energy, and professionalism. Augmenting her curatorial efforts at the museum were a number of divisions and staff members, including Ms. Stofflet's assistant, Carol Caves, Deputy Director Jane Rice, Registrar Louis Goldich, Head of Installation and Design Darcie Fohrman, Head of Publications and Sales David Hewitt, Public Information Officer Barbara Fleming, Assistant to the Registrar Anne Streicher,

***"You hush up your mouth!"* from *Yertle the Turtle and Other Stories,* 1958 [140].**

Curatorial Assistant, Exhibitions, Rebecca Sanders, Construction Supervisor Danielle Hanrahahn, Graphics Coordinator Deena Blaylock, and Development Associate Rosetta Sciacca Ellis, each of whom coordinated numerous aspects of the project with consummate skill and devotion. We are indebted to the many lenders and institutions that generously shared their collections of Dr. Seuss drawings, sketches, and memorabilia, particularly the University Research Library, University of California, Los Angeles, and David Zeidberg, head of the Department of Special Collections, Kayla Landesman, assistant to the manuscript librarian and cataloguer of the Theodor Geisel Collection, and Simon Elliott of Reader Services.

We gratefully acknowledge the assistance of Curator Gary Yarrington and Registrar Pat Burchfield of the Lyndon Baines Johnson Library and Museum, Austin, Texas. Sherry Gerstein and Charles Selden of Random House likewise aided us in our research. Grateful acknowledgments are extended also to Jed Mattes of International Creative Management, Kris Gilmore of the Stoorza Company, and Letitia Burns O'Connor and Dana Levy of Perpetua Press for their insights and hard work in the development of the exhibition catalogue. Additional thanks to Michael Arthur for his photography.

The many patrons in San Diego and around the country who rallied behind this project and supported its various components are gratefully appreciated. Allied-Signal Inc., a corporation with a distinguished record of support for the arts, provided a generous grant for the national presentation of this exhibition. The James S. Copley Foundation, in recognition of the important role of the arts in the community and in expression of their high regard for the contributions of Ted Geisel, provided a major grant for the exhibition. Cecil and Ida Green continue their long and supportive relationship with Ted Geisel in recognizing this project.

Especially noteworthy was the effort of Joseph Hibben, a friend of both Ted Geisel and the San Diego Museum of Art, who proposed the project and, with his wife Ingrid, supported it with funding as a reflection of their admiration for the artist and his work.

Like most major exhibition projects, *Dr. Seuss from Then to Now* would not have been possible without the generosity and commitment of corporate sponsors. Home Federal has continued a long tradition of supporting arts by underwriting this tour, and we are indebted to its enlightened management.

We are delighted to present this exhibition for all of Dr. Seuss's countless admirers across the country—and we welcome once again all who have ever spent an afternoon with a Who, a Grinch, or a Zax to the wonderful, wacky world of the Good Doctor.

Steven L. Brezzo
Director
San Diego Museum of Art

Introduction

For baby boomers he was the poet laureate. Into a world of Crayola crayons, construction-paper pilgrims, and asphalt playgrounds, Dr. Seuss introduced an adventure of rhyme and image with the power to alleviate our boredom, challenge our imaginations, and even shape our young lives.

I first made the acquaintance of Dr. Seuss on a dreary afternoon, amidst an unruly crowd of second graders, facing the prospect of a rained-out recess. Typically we greeted the crisis with behavior that bordered on anarchy. Miss Blakemere's futile attempts to calm the fray were unsuccessful until as a last resort she hoisted the white flag of a story hour.

Our wary group, weaned on Superman comics and Burma Shave signs, settled in with trepidation, prepared for another installment of the dreaded "Once upon a time."

> The sun did not shine
> It was too wet to play.
> So we sat in the house
> All that cold, cold, wet day.

Miss Blakemere paused and looked up, savoring the moment. A sly smile preceded a delightful falsetto:

> We looked!
> Then we saw him step in on the mat!
> We looked!
> And we saw him!
> The Cat in the Hat!

We were hooked. As she paraded up and down the aisles, displaying the illustrations to us as she read, we clambered over one another, vying for a better view. The cat was comically rendered, with a Chaplinesque savoir faire, and his companions, devoid of the traditional cherubic attributes of kiddie-lit characters, looked impish and familiar.

The story captivated us—an uninvited cat in a tilted stovepipe hat, who created mayhem as well as magic; goofy little creatures called Thing One and Thing Two, who ransacked the house with aplomb; and the rhyming goldfish, whose Greek-chorus conscience the children warily ignored. It all ended in a breathless race to put everything back in place before mom got home from her errands.

By the time Miss Blakemere closed the book, we were transfixed. Intuitively, she understood what had transpired; a significant moment in our rowdy existence had just passed, and none of us had any inkling of how important that story was to become.

I was, like children everywhere that fall, being introduced to a new and important wonder of the childhood world: an author who neither preached nor conspired against honest-to-gosh childhood whims; a writer-illustrator whose stories addressed the wild and woolly illogic of real kids longing to immerse themselves in books that tickled their boundless fancies and lifted their literary spirits. It was as if my schoolmates and I had just made the acquaintance of a new and exciting secret playmate; a buddy who, although not always scrupulously well mannered according to the tenets of the adult world, could be counted on to provide a fantastic refuge of wacky characters, convoluted logic, and silly vocabulary. And miraculously, grown-ups not only stood by while we reveled in the books, they actually condoned the stuff!

Here, at last was "children's literature" without the timidity and oversentimentality of traditional works yet which conformed to the features of classic picture-book narratives. The stories were replete with action involving

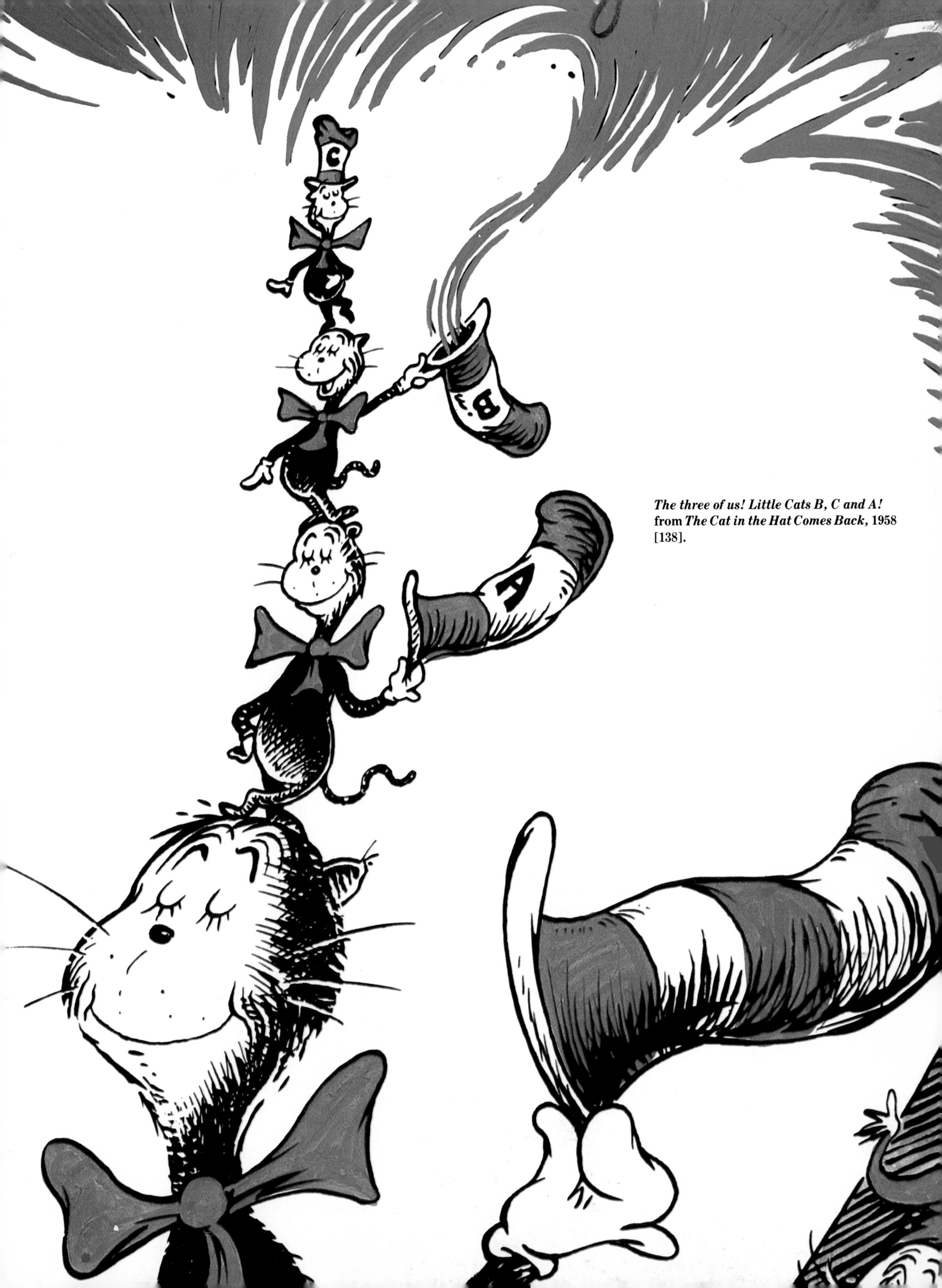
C
B
A

The three of us! Little Cats B, C and A!
from *The Cat in the Hat Comes Back,* 1958
[138].

wonderfully endearing characters, they contained frequent changes in imaginative and colorful scenery and were sustained by a narrative that led the reader in a comfortably symmetrical literary direction. This, however, was an assessment that I would apply to the works many years later. To me and my childhood lit-mates, first discovering the joys of independent reading, Dr. Seuss immediately became a synonym for lively and fanciful adventures.

To all of us there appeared to be no end to the author's ingenuity: Greeches and Grinches, Sneetches and Whos, an entire universe of nonsense gleefully engaged our minds and expanded our budding vocabularies. The stories, like our lives at that age, were masterworks of appealing improvisation—wonderful flights of ingenuity, humor, and sparkling word play. Logic be damned, the author seemed to suggest, let's just have some fun.

The books were piled in our rooms next to oversized catcher's mitts and the assorted flotsam of youth: dog-eared baseball cards, plastic kachina dolls from Uncle Ellwood's trip to Niagara Falls, Bazooka bubble-gum wrappers. The volumes were splattered with grape-juice stains and cookie crumbs, their corners gnawed by the teething puppy, but they were cherished, the first books we ever cared about. We coveted them and bragged about our growing collections. "Whaddiya get for Christmas, Calvin? *I* got a Bozo punching bag, a Howdy Doody wash-mitt, a dart gun, and a coupla' Dr. Seuss books!" Cate-

gorizing books in the same treasured universe as sports gear and bubble gum was to us of no small intellectual consequence; in a real, but subtle way Dr. Seuss had become part of our coming of age.

Why were these works so important to us? Perhaps because Dr. Seuss accepted for a fact our own youthful artistic openness. We were longing for stories that imposed no limitations on our creativity and imagination. Like us, Dr. Seuss explored a boundless terrain of silliness and illogic. It was as if he, like all of us at Albert Einstein Elementary School, continually demanded of the reigning authorities, "Who made up these rules, anyhow?" Dr. Seuss had become in a rare and special way one of us. Without ever meeting him, we knew that here at last was a grown-up who probably hated carrots, napped in the afternoon, doodled in the margins, and secretly sported a skinned knee.

As children who grew up on the white-bread escapades of Dick and Jane, we were utterly amazed at the originality and shimmering spontaneity of these new tales. These were stories told with a sense of inspired nonsense and delicate warmth. The Cat in the Hat was a real and joyful pain in the neck; Horton was a nice old elephant but dreadfully slow on the uptake; the Grinch was every grouchy grown-up we had ever known; and Mulberry Street was all a baby-boomer neighborhood should be.

The books brought our families closer together in ways only shared expe-

Yawn Song **from** ***The Cat in the Hat Song Book,*** **1967 [177].**

I CAN READ IT ALL BY MYSELF
Beginner Books
Beginner Books
A DIVISION OF RANDOM HOUSE, INC.
Box 1924, La Jolla, California
T. S. Geisel, PRESIDENT
Poodle with his left hand
Camel with his right hand.
...with his left big toe.

Preliminary drawings, *The Cat in the Hat Song Book,* n.d. [182].

riences between parents and children can. They had a downright elixirlike effect on grown-ups. As children, we had grown accustomed to the predictable routine of adults reading to us from our family's private library stock. Dads tended to opt for a few bedtime paragraphs from *Treasure Island*, while moms (this was the fifties, remember) invariably selected another installment of the Oz saga or a few cloying chapters from *The Pony That Kept a Secret*. There was little drama in these renditions, and we usually dozed off, as intended, after only a few sentences.

Dr. Seuss, however, instigated a bedtime revolution. His playful language and captivating story lines turned once formal, mundane readings by our parents into wildly improvisational, side-splitting dramatic presentations. Moms altered their soothing voices to approximate the call of a Lorax; dads made noises like Sneetches and pretended to hatch an elephant's egg; and we joined in the silliness, cavorting through those magical moments when all barriers disappeared and grown-ups became playmates and partners in fun.

Left alone, we would cuddle up in a couch or lie on a comfortable stretch of carpet and gaze at the pages for hours. As an illustrator, Dr. Seuss was a self-proclaimed interloper. The man behind the Quick, Henry, the Flit! advertising campaign, he had achieved a kind of cult status among the kids of my neighborhood. To his peers, Dr. Seuss was an artistic eccentric, a position he did little to

It all starts with Dr. Seuss
© 1955 Dr. Seuss

challenge when he admitted (with what was surely a twinkle in his eye), that he "just never learned to draw." To those of us in the second grade, he was a veritable old master. Like his stories, his text illustrations were a poke in the eye of literary and artistic convention.

It all starts with Dr. Seuss, **button, 1955 [238].**

His expressive creatures and wondrous locales cascaded across pages and seemed to hop over bindings. As readers, we zoomed in and out of scenes and screeched through evolving scenarios. Every page was a new and stimulating visual adventure with an endless variety of amusing creatures and expressionistic sets. Sam-I-Am served platters of green eggs and ham; moss-covered, three-handled gredunzas were pursued by a cat in a fedora; Mr. Krinklebein, a talking goldfish, resided in a bowl overseen by wildly coiffed Thing One and Thing Two; and wockets filled our pockets.

There was certainly a moral sense to the books, but it was neither deliberately apparent nor overly pedantic. We got the message nonetheless; characters discovered the nature of racial prejudice, greed, disdain for the unusual, and the perils posed by uninvited guests. Lessons were usually presented in a subtle manner, but the stories avoided piety and solemnity to resolve themselves in a consistently upbeat way.

Today most of us who lived with and loved these stories are voracious readers. Books clutter our homes and offices and weigh down our luggage when we travel. We crowd bookstores and eagerly await reviews of new works. We are unabashedly enthusiastic readers, thanks to our earliest encounters with books that thrilled, entertained, and instructed us; stories filled with ingenious characters, wondrous images, and imaginative language.

Thanks to Dr. Seuss, and a supporting cast of insightful teachers and clever parents, we emerged from our collective childhood with imaginations enhanced, an enduring enjoyment of words, and a sense of visual literacy.

We were lucky to have encountered Dr. Seuss, and, now that I think of it, we were fortunate to have experienced a few rained-out recesses too.

Steven L. Brezzo
Director
San Diego Museum of Art

Dr. Seuss from THEN to NOW

So that's what the Birthday Bird does in Katroo from *Happy Birthday to You!*, 1959 [147].

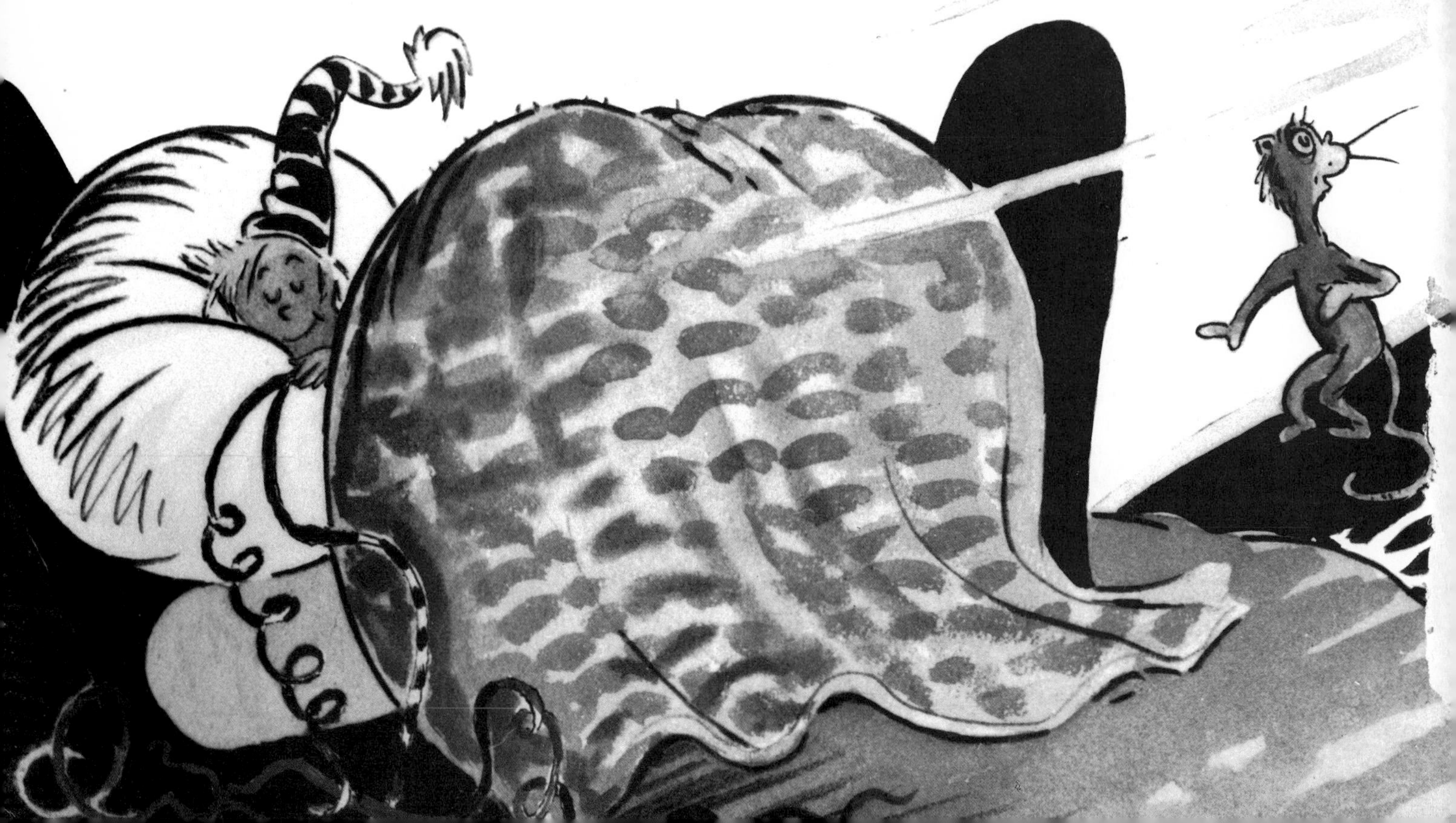

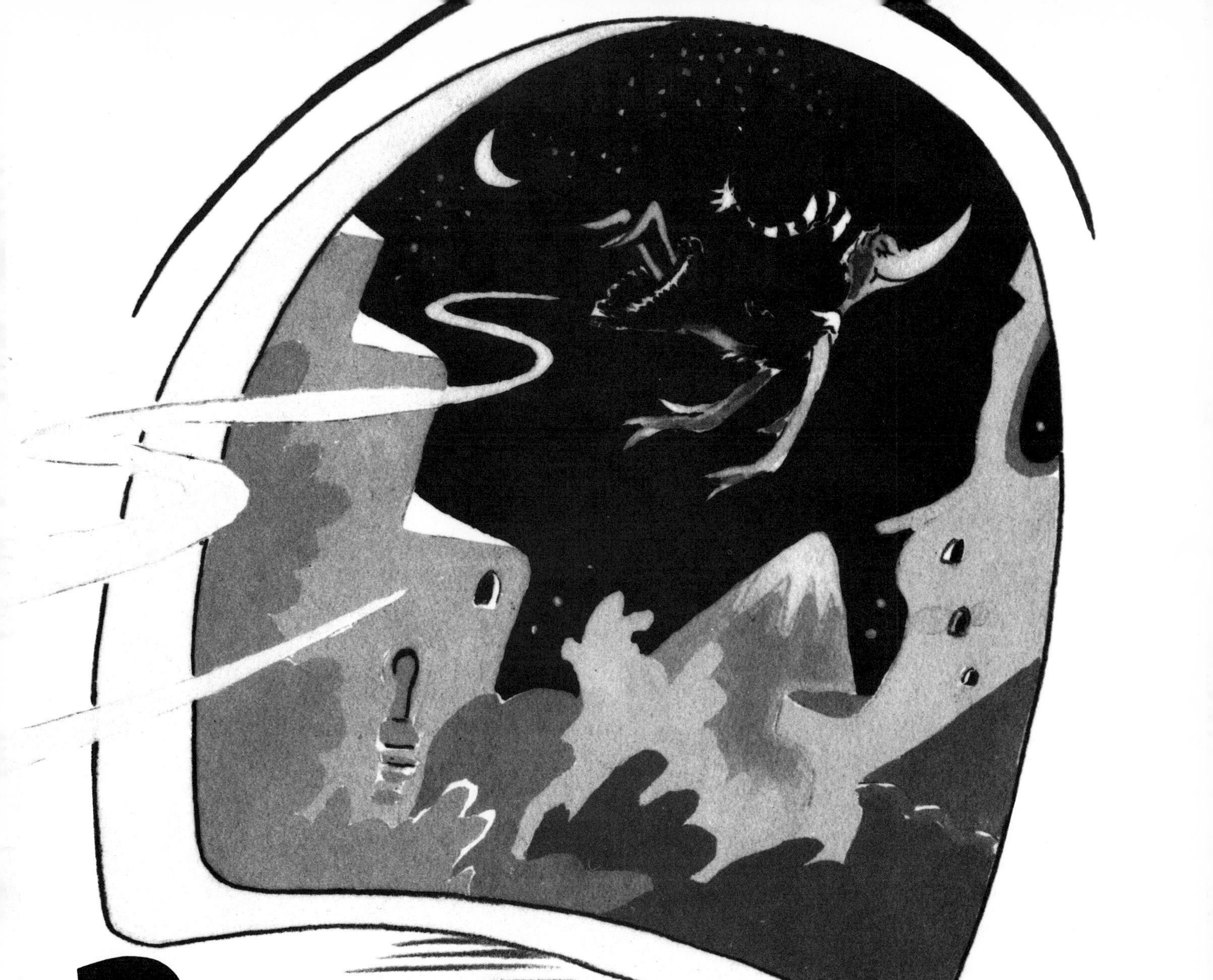

Bartholomew Cubbins, the Lorax, Sam-I-Am, the Cat in the Hat... three generations of children all over the world have grown up loving these characters created by Dr. Seuss. More than one hundred million Dr. Seuss books have been purchased by parents, grandparents, and children in Japan, Israel, Norway, Sweden, Denmark, Germany, Holland, Italy, Brazil, and the countries of the British Commonwealth. *Green Eggs and Ham* (1960) is the third-largest selling book in the English language. Ever. *The Butter Battle Book* (1984), supposedly for children, set a world's record by appearing for six months on the *New York Times* adult best- seller list. Dr. Seuss is definitely a household name, but who is he? And where has he been from then to now?

He wasn't always Dr. Seuss. Born in Springfield, Massachusetts, in 1904, he was known as Theodor Geisel until he became involved in a minor infraction of the rules while attending Dartmouth College. To maintain his post as editor-in-chief of the college humor magazine *Jack-o-Lantern*, under the watchful eye of the dean, he began to sign his works with his middle name, Seuss. The title of doctor came later, after he dropped out of Oxford University. Not wanting to disappoint his father by arriving home without a doctorate, he simply annexed *Dr.* to his middle name. Except for various appellations assumed during the 1920s—such as Theo Seuss 2nd, Dr. Theophrastus Seuss,

JUDGE
MARCH 23, 1929
PRICE 15 CENTS
JUNGLE NUMBER
Dr. Seuss

Judge
JUNE
1933
PRICE 15 CENTS
20 Cents in Canada
Dr. Seuss

TECHNOCRACY
NUMBER OF
JUDGE
PRICE 15 CENTS
20 Cents in Canada
MARCH
1933
Dr. Seuss

Life
MAY
15 CENTS
IN CANADA 20¢
"I know, my dear, but that's NOTHING compared to having an egg!"
Dr. Seuss

Covers, ***Judge***, 1929 [5a] 1933, [5b, 5c].

I know, my dear, but that's **NOTHING** ***compared to having an egg!*****, cover, *Life*, c. 1929–30 [14].**

Dr. Seuss

ALPS
T. Seuss

Financial Note: Goat Milk is Higher than Ever.

Financial Note, **c. 1930s [20c] and 1925 [1].**

and Dr. Theodophilus Seuss, Ph.D., I.Q., H_2SO_4—the name Dr. Seuss has been used by Theodor Geisel ever since. A string of honorary doctorates, most recently from Princeton University, merely adds an academic patina to the reputation of the world's best-known doctor.

Although Dr. Seuss's characters inhabit the imagination rather than the realm of personal experience, a few clues to the life of Theodor Geisel can be found in his books. *If I Ran the Zoo* (1950) surely relates to his father, who was a zookeeper, and for whom the dedication in *If I Ran the Circus* (1956) reads: "This book is for my dad, Big Ted of Springfield, the finest man I'll ever know."

Dr. Seuss, who claims to be a self-taught artist, had a drawing lesson once. When he turned his paper upside down to study the composition, the teacher walked by and said, "Ted, real artists don't turn their paper upside down." He never returned to the class.

While briefly attending Lincoln College, Oxford University, he kept a rather ordinary notebook with a black cover and metal rings. On its unlined pages he drew animals, a woman dressed for golf, and members of his literature class. One student, Helen Palmer, looked over his shoulder and said, "You're not very interested in the lectures." He thought she was right, so he left the university and traveled through Europe in 1926–27.

Europe between the wars was a glittery place described by Geisel's Ox-

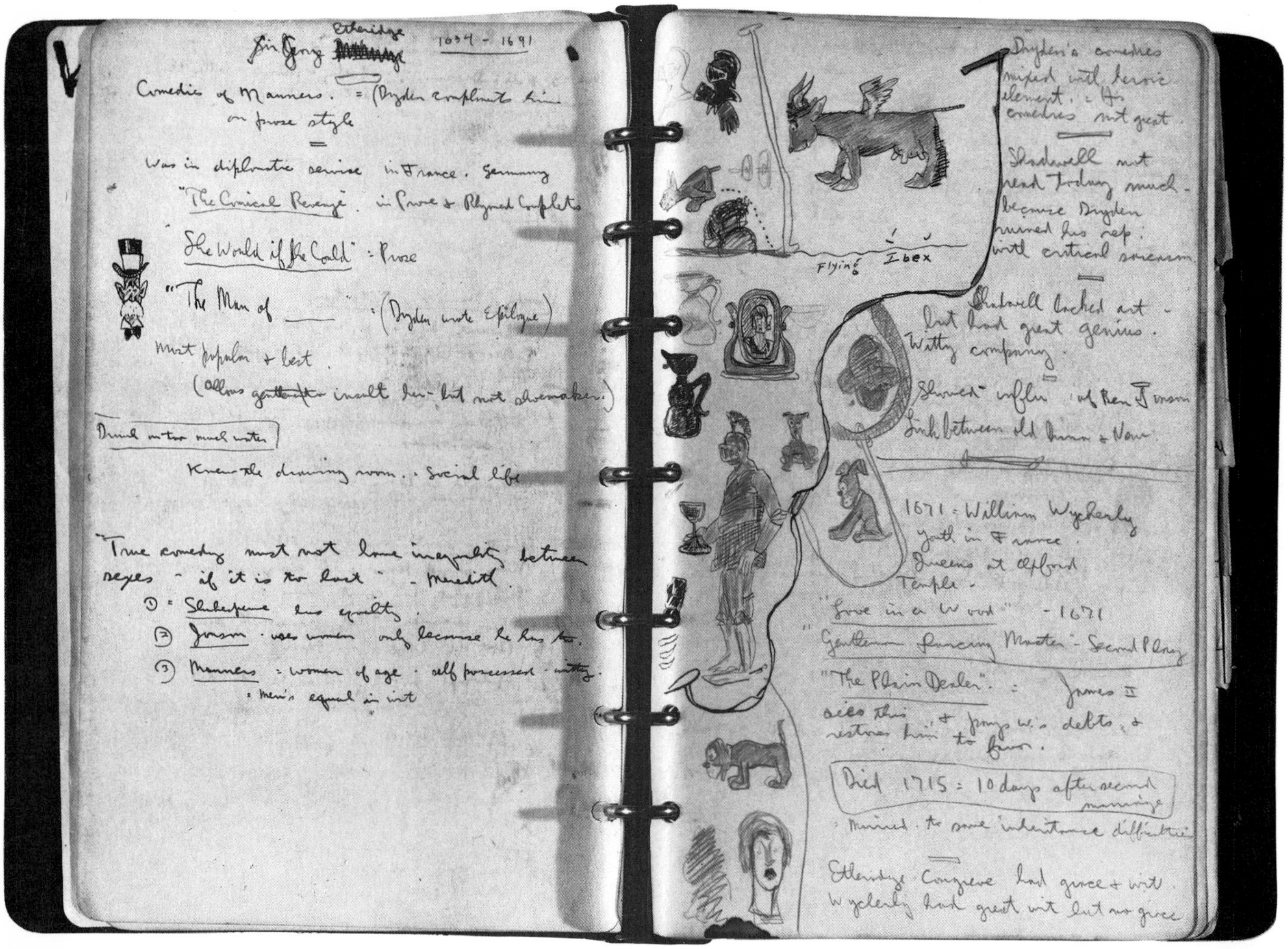
1634 - 1691
Comedies of Manners
Flying Ibex
1671 = William Wycherly
"Love in a Wood" - 1671
"The Plain Dealer"
Died 1715 = 10 days after second marriage

Notebook of Theodor S. Geisel, Lincoln College, Oxford University, 1925–26 [3].

Hill No. I.
Hill No. 2
Hill No. 3
Hill No. 4
Hill No. 5
Hill No. 6
Hill No. 7

***Romulus and Remus*, c. 1925–27 [4a].**

Dragon, after Piero di Cosimo, c. 1925–27 [4c]; _Perseus Frees Andromeda_ by Piero di Cosimo. Uffizi Gallery, Florence.

ford contemporary Evelyn Waugh in his satirical novel of the 1920s, *Vile Bodies*:

> Masked parties, Savage parties, Victorian parties, Greek parties, Wild West parties, Russian parties, Circus parties, parties where one had to dress as somebody else, almost naked parties in St. John's Wood, parties in flats and studios and houses and ships and hotels and night clubs, in windmills and swimming-baths, tea parties at school where one ate muffins and meringues and tinned crab, parties at Oxford where one drank brown sherry and smoked Turkish cigarettes, dull dances in London and comic dances in Scotland and disgusting dances in Paris—all that succession and repetition of massed humanity.[1]

Geisel saw it all and even produced some drawings during what he now calls his "Roman and Florentine Period." These fractured bits of Roman history include a Seussian version of Romulus and Remus, a group of vestal virgins on the forum, and a dragon, drawn directly from the central monster in *Perseus Frees Andromeda* by Piero di Cosimo in the Uffizi Gallery, Florence. This was the last time that art history was to intrude on Geisel's work.

Back in New York in 1927 he must have found the same between-the-wars euphoria, the same world of parties, the same subjects for satire that attracted many writers of the period. Now he says, "When I think about the twenties, I realize that so much of my work was about drinking." His exotic animals sampling the cocktail-party circuit were an uncommon subject for car-

QUICK, HENRY, THE FLIT!
A STANCO PRODUCT
FLIT
Kills
Moths
Mosquitoes
Flies
Bed Bugs
Roaches
Ants
Dr. Seuss
LOW PRICES
FLIT KILLS FLIES AND MOSQUITOES

"Quick, Henry!
the
FLIT"
REG. U. S. PAT. OFF.
Dr. Seuss
FLIT
Kills
Flies
Mosquitoes
Moths

Quick, Henry, the Flit!, posters for Flit advertising campaign, 1941 [32] and 1930 [26b]; ***Foiled by Essolube, a jigsaw melodrama,*** Standard Oil Company of New Jersey advertising campaign, c. 1930s [45].

Essolube
FOILED BY ESSOLUBE
Dr. Seuss

Seuss Navy

Seuss Navy Flag, **Standard Oil Company of New Jersey advertising campaign, c. 1936 [43];** ***An Ancient News Picture,*** **Flit advertising campaign, n.d. [28a].**

toons at the time. A genius at creating a page crowded with images, spiced with a telling line of dialogue, he insightfully recorded the mores of society in popular humor magazines. These cartoons, with their illustrative complexity, suggest his later achievements to the careful observer. Although he may appear to be a frivolous chronicler of café society, he also expresses a political sensibility in his work, from the earliest Dartmouth drawings of the 1920s to the explicit, political cartoons of the early 1940s.

Characters and captions appear and reappear in various contexts. The humorous name Thidwick, later applied to a big-hearted moose, is first used in *Pentellic Bilge for Bennett Cerf's Birthday* eight years before it appeared in a book.[2] The 1925 mountaintop goat from the Dartmouth *Jack-o-Lantern* has a caption of socio-political significance: "*Financial Note*: Goat Milk is Higher than Ever." This image and message reappears in a series of 1930s calendar-art drawings. As early as 1929, a precursor of Horton, the elephant, appears on the cover of the magazine *Judge*. Ask Ted Geisel if he keeps a notebook of ideas and he won't answer you, but these early gems glimmer among his drawings, waiting to be developed into a story or book.

For *Judge* magazine sometime during the late 1920s he drew a cartoon with a medieval castle, armored knight, and dragon, which he captioned, "Medieval tenant: 'Darn it all, another Dragon. And just after I'd sprayed the

Another Big FLIT Year!
REG. U.S. PAT. OFF.
Quick, Henry! the "FLIT"
SEUSS

Foil the Karbo-nockus!
Essolube
5-STAR MOTOR OIL
Forms less carbon
AT STANDARD STATIONS
Dr. Seuss

Foil the Moto-raspus!
Essolube
5-STAR MOTOR OIL
Fights Friction
AT STANDARD STATIONS

Another Big Flit Year!, booklet for Flit advertising campaign, 1931 [29]; *Foil the Karbo-nockus!* and *Foil the Moto-raspus!*, posters for Standard Oil Company of New Jersey advertising campaign, 1933 [39b–c]

We're lost if we steer by the Great North Bear; steer by the Small South Whoosis! **from *Life*, c. 1929–30 [15b]; *Animals Every Student Loves* by Dr. Theodophilus Seuss, Ph.D., I.Q., H_2SO_4 from *College Humor*, c. 1929–30 [17c].**

ALKY
Dr. Seuss

whole castle with Flit!' " The wife of a Flit account executive saw the drawing and implored her husband to hire the talented artist. He did, Seuss developed a successful ad campaign for Flit, and the resulting income provided financial stability for his marriage in 1927 to Helen Palmer, whose observant remark at Oxford had changed his life forever. Seuss also created other advertising campaigns for Standard Oil Company of New Jersey, Schaefer Bock Beer, Ford Motor Company, Atlas Products, New Departure Bearings, NBC Radio, and later Holly Sugar. These corporations never imposed their identity on the work of Dr. Seuss. Although his familiar signature often appears in the ads, his style is immediately recognizable without it. Even the slogans are Seussian, appropriate for a man who has been described as a master of comic doggerel, for example, "If Flit can knock / *this* monster stiff / mere bugs and such / won't last *one whiff!*" Or, for Esso, "Foil the Moto-raspus! Foil the Zero-doccus! Foil the Karbo-nockus!" The Flit campaign was wildly successful. Books of Flit cartoons were published: *Flit Cartoons As They Have Appeared in Magazines throughout the Country* (vol. 1, 1929, and 2, 1930) and *Another Big Flit Year!* (1931). After a period of freelancing, which he now describes as a "hellish, confused, mixed-up activity to scratch out a living during the Depression," Dr. Seuss was on his way to a promising career. Yet even the despair of being underemployed in the 1930s is given the Seuss comic style in "The Sad, Sad Story of the Obsks,"

AND TO THINK
THAT I SAW IT ON
MULBERRY STREET
MULBERRY ST.
By Dr. Seuss
Cover, *And to Think That I Saw It on Mulberry Street*, 1937.

With a roar of its motor an airplane appears
And dumps out confetti while everyone cheers.
And that makes a story that's really not bad!
But it still could be better. Suppose that I add . . . .

Spread from *And to Think That I Saw It on Mulberry Street,* 1937.

an unpublished, four-page illustrated novelette, written in 1938 on the occasion of his leaving Standard Oil. The entire text reads:

A flock of Obsks
From down in Nobsks

Hiked up to Bobsks
To look for Jobsks.

Then back to Nobsks
With sighs and Sobsks...

There were, in Bobsks,
No jobs for Obsks.[3]

The Obsk appeared again in *If I Ran the Zoo.*

Did the advertising business provide sufficient creative opportunity for an artist of Geisel's wit, imagination, and scope? He must have had some doubts. Certainly the satirical spirit of the 1920s was at work when he produced a series of drawings called The Advertising Business at a Glance. Among the titles are *The Man with an Idea, The Account Executive* (in his shorts, with brief case, jumping hurdles in the office), and *"Now Let's Really Analyze that Humorous Advertising."* The man who once described himself as an amateur mummy digger was still seeking other options.

Drawing from *The Seven Lady Godivas*, 1939.

Lulu Godiva, after being kicked by her horse, records her Horse Truth in the book and leaves the place forever from *The Seven Lady Godivas*, 1939 [78].

Ted Geisel got the idea to write children's books when he illustrated *Boners*, a collection of schoolboy howlers, in 1931. He did not want to be limited to illustrations and developed his first full-length children's book from a piece of ship's stationery, which he had covered with ideas and phrases: "A stupid horse and wagon... horse and chariot... chariot pulled by flying cat... flying cat pulling at Viking ship... Viking ship sailing up a volcano... Volcano blowing hearts diamonds & clubs... I saw a giant eight miles tall... who took the cards 52 in all... And this is a story that no one can beat... I saw it all happen on Mulberry Street."[4] In 1963 he described the incident.

> These are the first words I ever wrote in the field of writing for children. I put them down in the bar of the M.S. *Kungsholm*, sometime during the summer of 1936. I wrote them for only one reason. I was trying to keep my mind off the storm that was going on. (The rhythm of the rudimentary refrain came from the beat of the ship's motors.) This rhythm persisted in my head for about a week after I was off the ship and, probably as psycho-therapy, I began developing the theme. It turned into my first Juvenile... *And to Think That I Saw It on Mulberry Street.* Although I knew nothing about children's books it sounded pretty good, so I decided to get it published. It was rejected by twenty-eight publishing

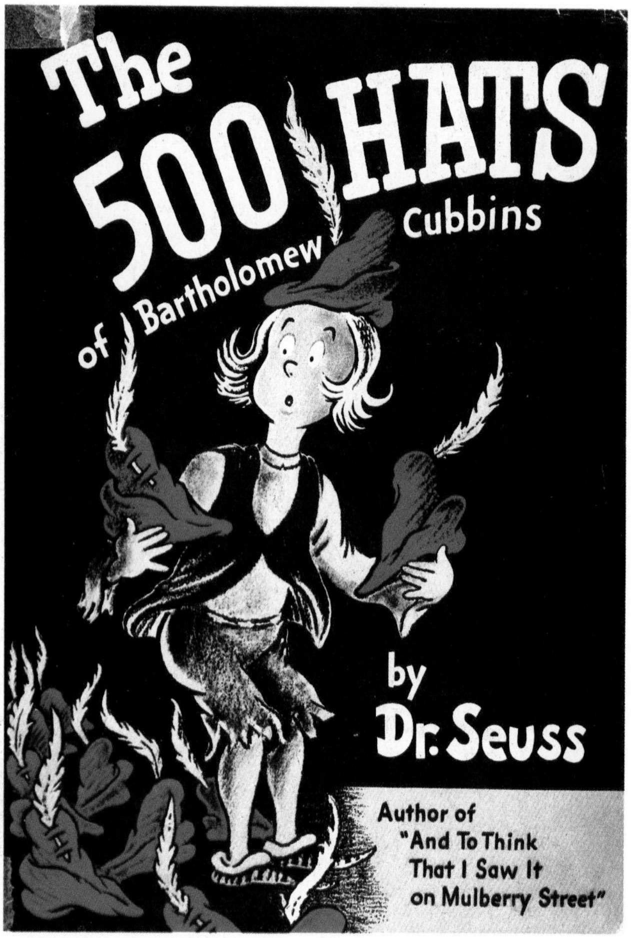
The
500 HATS
of Bartholomew Cubbins
by
Dr. Seuss
Author of
"And To Think
That I Saw It
on Mulberry Street"

ふしぎな
500のぼうし
シュース博士著
大森武男訳

Presentation copy, 1938 [79], Japanese edition, 1949 [80], and *He was wearing the most beautiful hat that had ever been seen in the Kingdom of Didd* from *The 500 Hats of Bartholomew Cubbins,* 1981 [87].

HORTON HEARS A WHO!
By
Dr. Seuss

Horton Hatches the Egg
Dr. Seuss

Presentation copy, *Horton Hears a Who!,* 1954 [112]; dust jacket proof, *Horton Hatches the Egg,* 1940 [91].

> houses before the twenty-ninth, Vanguard Press, agreed to take a chance on bringing it out. The main reason given by the other publishing houses for rejecting it was: it was too different from other children's books then on the market.[5]

Today he says, "It was finally accepted when an old Dartmouth friend who had become a children's book publisher that morning bumped into me on the street. See, everything has to do with luck."

Mulberry Street (1937) did well, but Seuss's next book was geared toward an adult audience. "We charged two dollars for *The Seven Lady Godivas,*" he says now. "It was the Depression. Nobody had two dollars." The idea for the book, which centers on the discovery through humorous adventure of Horse Truths, such as "Don't look a gift horse in the mouth," by each Godiva sister, was a good one. Long out of print until it was reissued in 1987, *The Seven Lady Godivas* (1939) begins with these words:

> Foreword. History has treated no one so shabbily as it has the name of Godiva. Today Lady Godiva brings to mind a shameful picture—a big blonde nude trotting around town on a horse. In the background of this picture, there is always Peeping Tom, an illicit snooper with questionable intentions. The author feels

I'll sit on your egg and I'll try not to break it from ***Horton Hatches the Egg,*** 1940 [93].

They laughed and they laughed. Then they all ran away **from *Horton Hatches the Egg,* 1940 [94].**

that the time has come to speak: *There was not one; there were Seven Lady Godivas, and their nakedness actually was not a thing of shame. So far as Peeping Tom is concerned, he never really peeped. "Peeping" was merely an old family name and Tom and his six brothers bore it with pride.* A beautiful story of love, honor, and scientific achievement that has too long been gathering dust in the archives. Dr. Seuss. Coventry, 1939.[6]

The next few years saw the creation of two of Dr. Seuss's best-loved characters, Bartholomew Cubbins in *The 500 Hats of Bartholomew Cubbins* (1938) and *Bartholomew and the Oobleck* (1949) and Horton the elephant in *Horton Hatches the Egg* (1940) and *Horton Hears a Who!* (1954). Each of these characters has also appeared in lesser-known short stories, "The Royal Housefly and Bartholomew Cubbins" in *Junior Catholic Messenger* (1950) and "Horton and the Kwuggerbug" in *Redbook* (1951). Bartholomew Cubbins, a rare human hero in the world of Seuss, is beset with problems that get him into trouble with a king. In *The 500 Hats* he saves his own neck when he is unable to remove a multitude of hats in recognition of the king. The stream of hats ends with "the most beautiful hat that had ever been seen in the Kingdom of Didd," which the relieved Bartholomew exchanges for the king's favor. In *Bartholomew and the Oobleck* he appears as a humanitarian who saves the entire kingdom from the gooey, green, destructive oobleck after the irresponsible monarch

Hejji
By Dr. Seuss
BEYOND JAGGED PEAKS LIES THE LAND OF BAAKO HIDDEN—UNKNOWN. SHUT OFF FROM OUR WORLD BY MOUNTAINS SO HIGH THAT MOST BIRDS CANNOT FLY THEM. ONLY THE BAAKINESE EAGLE CAN SOAR SO HIGH. HE HAS TO TAXI OTHERS ACROSS!
NATURE HAS STRANGE WAYS IN THE MOUNTAINS OF BAAKO. IN LAKES ON OLD VOLCANO TOPS, WHALES SPLASH AND SPOUT... 10,000 LEAGUES FROM THE NEAREST SEA!
INTO THIS LAND COMES HEJJI A STRANGER
WHAT A COUNTRY! TURTLES THAT GALLOP!
WHEW! TWO GOATS THAT WEAR ONE BEARD BETWEEN THEM!
AND HERE'S SOME STUNT, A FLOWER BROADCASTING MUSIC
BY THE MOON'S RIB! HE'S PLUCK'D THE TRUMPET FLOWER OF BAAKO!
SEIZE HIM!
WE'LL DRAGGLE HIM BEFORE THE MIGHTY ONE!
THE MIGHTY ONE HAS PROMISED THAT FLOWER TO HIS FAIR ONE!
SHUT UP, YOU NOISY VEGETABLE! YOU'VE GOT ME INTO A FINE MESS!
IT WILL GO HARD WITH THIS YOUNG FOREIGN FOOL!
HARD INDEED! THE MIGHTY ONE IS IN A DARK, DARK MOOD!
WHAT FATE AWAITS HEJJI BEYOND THESE TOWERING GATES OF BAAKO!
4-7

Hejji, **Sunday, April 7, 1935 [18a].**

It was in the throne room that Bartholomew found him from *Bartholomew and the Oobleck,* 1949 [105].

caused the mess by ordering his magicians to think up some new and different weather.

Horton is a self-sacrificing elephant who sits on a nest while its owner, the flighty Maysie, goes off to Florida for some sunshine. He utters the now classic line, "I meant what I said, and I said what I meant... an elephant's faithful—one hundred percent!" He is rewarded at the end when a small elephant with wings cracks its way out of the egg. In *Horton Hears a Who!* the eponymous elephant saves the tiny Whos of Who-ville from destruction by the insensitive Wickersham gang. The Seuss settings are faraway kingdoms, and the villains and plights are known to all.

Between Seuss the freelance artist of the 1930s and Seuss the full-fledged storybook author of later decades, there was a lesser-known Seuss, the political cartoonist of the newspaper *PM* in the 1940s. Seuss had been a cartoonist before. In 1935 he was hired briefly by the Hearst newspapers to draw *Hejji,* a series described in *The Smithsonian Collection of Newspaper Comics* as a "wonderful example of what happened when Dr. Seuss's gorgeous lunacy moved briefly into comics."[7] Seuss describes his departure from the newspaper: "A telegram came from William Randolph Hearst saying fire the last three people you hired. I was one of them, so it was the end of that career. It's just as well. I don't know where the story would have gone next." *PM* cir-

A GREAT SATIRIST . . . WHO CAN CHASE . . . AN ENEMY TO . . .

Dr. Seuss, I presume..

Here's a new kind of Editorial Cartoon which will help your editorial page sparkle . . .

"Sis! Boom! Bah! Rah!
Sis! Boom! Bah! Rah!
Million! Billion! Trillion! Rillion!
Sis! Boom! Bah!"
RUSSIANS KILLED
9,128,275
10,200,777
GOEBBELS
Dr. Seuss

PETAIN
Dr. Seuss

"Put your arm up like this, and your troubles are over . . ."

THE GREAT U.S. SIDE SHOW
AMERICA FIRST
"And on this platform, folks, those most perplexing people…the Lads with the Siamese Beard! Unrelated by blood, they are joined in a manner that mystifies the mightiest minds in the land!"

Time to get up and
Face the new day!
THE GRIM COLD FACTS
OUR WARM, WARM COT
Dr. Seuss

The ALIBI BOYS
That Favorite Song-and-Dance Team of the Democratic Nations
WE COULD OF
WE WOULD OF
WE SHOULD OF
Dr. Seuss

". . . and protect my beddie from the Communist Boogey Man!"
ANTI-RUSSIAN JITTERER
"Ain't that cute! Same prayer the Fuehrer taught me when I was a kid!"
Dr. Seuss

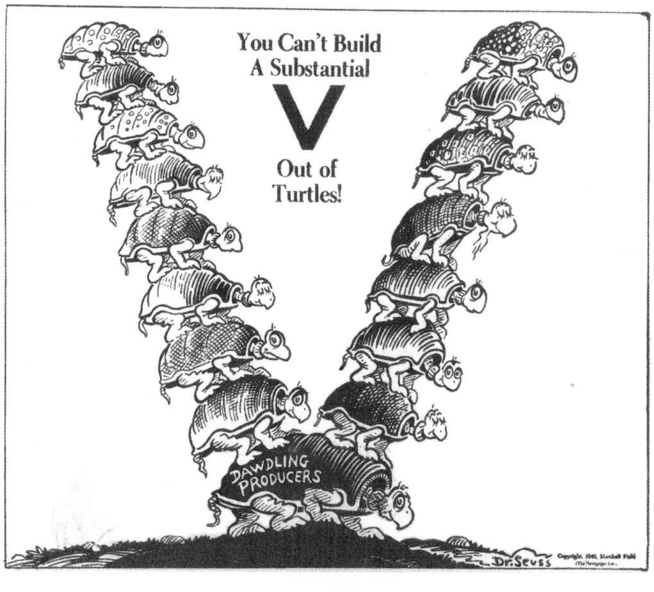

You Can't Build
A Substantial
V
Out of
Turtles!
DAWDLING PRODUCERS
Dr. Seuss

Political cartoons for *PM,* 1942 [47a, 49a, 48a, 54].

COVER AS QUICKLY...
AS HENRY CAN...
FLATTEN A FLEA!
"So you don't like my new Eskimo suit, SO WHAT!"
ICELAND
Dr. Seuss
HAF YOU A MATCH, JA?
U.S. PATROL
Dr. Seuss
CONSOLIDATED WORLD DAIRY A. HITLER, Prop.
The head eats . . .
. . . the rest gets milked
JUGO SLAVIA
ROMANIA
GREECE
AUSTRIA
BELGIUM
HOLLAND
DENMARK
NORWAY
POLAND
CZECHO SLOVAKIA
FRANCE
Dr. Seuss
Dr. SEUSS is the same and only Dr. Seuss of "Quick-Henry-the-Flit" fame
Write or Wire today for prices
PM
SYNDICATE
HARRY BAKER, Manager
PM SYNDICATE
NEW YORK CITY

Dr. Seuss, I Presume**, brochure circulated by** ***PM*****, c. 1942 [55].**

culated a brochure called *Dr. Seuss, I Presume,* in which the promotional blurb reads, "Here's a new kind of Editorial Cartoon which will help your editorial page sparkle . . . a great satirist . . . who can chase . . . an enemy to . . . cover as quickly . . . as Henry can . . . flatten a flea! Dr. SEUSS is the same and only Dr. Seuss of 'Quick-Henry-the-Flit' fame."[8]

As a wartime artist, Seuss could place real-life good guys and bad guys in his own imaginative milieu and had the latitude of a cartoonist to depict them in fanciful guises. Among his most frequent targets were Hitler, Mussolini, and the Japanese and on the home front isolationism, inflation, and racial inequality. This concern for political issues is not absent from his later work, and as a creator of children's books Seuss has found the opportunity to introduce such topics as totalitarianism (*Yertle the Turtle,* 1958), environmentalism (*The Lorax,* 1971), discrimination (*The Sneetches and Other Stories,* 1961), and the commercialization of holidays (*How the Grinch Stole Christmas!,* 1957).

McELLIGOT'S
POOL

Drawing for dust jacket [95] and *The kind that likes flowers* [98] from *McElligot's Pool*, 1947.

DR. SEUSS

THIDWICK
The
Big-Hearted Moose
By Dr. Seuss

Presentation copy, ***Thidwick the Big-Hearted Moose*, 1948 [99].**

In January 1943 Geisel was commissioned as a captain in the Information and Education division of the U.S. Army and sent to "Fort Fox" in Hollywood, California.

There, under the command of Colonel Frank Capra, he began, for the first time, to make pictures that moved.

While in uniform he headed the animation section of Capra's Signal Corps unit, which produced the famous *Why We Fight* series of indoctrination films.

He also wrote and produced his first live-action film, a two-reeler entitled *Your Job in Germany.* This film, which established the ground rules for troops in the occupation of Germany, was later released by Warner Brothers for public showing under the title *Hitler Lives.* It won an Academy Award in 1945 for best documentary short subject of the year.

After three years in Hollywood, Washington, and Europe, he left the service as a lieutenant colonel.

While Geisel continued to produce children's books, among them

IF I RAN
The
ZOO
By
Dr. Seuss

Presentation copy, *If I Ran the Zoo,* 1950 [106].

OBSK

I'll go and I'll hunt in my Skeegle-mobile **[107] and *I'll bring back an Obsk* from *If I Ran the Zoo,* 1950 [108].**

McElligot's Pool (1947), *Thidwick the Big-Hearted Moose* (1948), and *If I Ran the Zoo,* he also wrote but did not design *Gerald McBoing-Boing,* an animated cartoon about a boy who could only say *boing.* He is still pleased with it, claiming that "it started a revolution in animation." The film, narrated by Marvin Miller of the television series *The Millionaire,* received an Academy Award in 1951. Dr. Seuss's last Hollywood project was *The 5000 Fingers of Dr. T.* (1952), which he will only describe as the worst experience of his life. The drawings for the sets and costumes for *Dr. T.* rank among Dr. Seuss's most arcane and terrifying, rather as though all the magicians and evildoers of the Bartholomew Cubbins era had suddenly sprung into Technicolor, yet they retain a spontaneity of line and illustrate a belief in the stability of the universe, so characteristic of Dr. Seuss's work.

A turning point, not only in the career of Dr. Seuss but in the reading habits of American children, occurred in the late 1950s. Inspired by a thoughtful article by John Hersey in *Life* magazine, entitled "Why do Students Bog Down on the First R?," Seuss began to address the problem, which has since entered popular parlance as the why-Johnny-can't-read syndrome. Hersey's contention was that the schools were filled with "pallid primers" such as *Fun with Dick and Jane,* featuring "abnormally courteous, unnaturally clean boys and girls," that real children found them uninspiring, and that many bookstores

WELCOME

Welcome from ***The 5000 Fingers of Dr. T.***, 1952 [62d].

THE CAT
IN
THE
HAT
By Dr. Seuss
I CAN READ IT ALL BY MYSELF
Beginner Books

Cover from *The Cat in the Hat*, 1957

Then out of the box came Thing Two and Thing One! from *The Cat in the Hat*, 1957 [133].

THING 1
THING 2

Now look what you did! from *The Cat in the Hat,* 1957 [132].

displayed more attractive alternatives, the "jaunty juveniles," with "strange and wonderful animals and children who behave naturally, i.e., sometimes misbehave."[10] Seuss's answer was *The Cat in the Hat*. By enhancing everyday situations with irresistible imaginary characters and telling the tales with cleverly rhymed, easily recognizable words, Seuss gave control of learning to read back to children, while providing wit, charm, comic verse, and a surprise on every page. *The Cat in the Hat* was so successful that Random House, publisher of all the Dr. Seuss books since 1937, created a special division, Beginner Books, with the Cat in the Hat as the logo and Dr. Seuss as president of the division. Other Cat in the Hat books followed: *The Cat in the Hat Comes Back* (1958), *The Cat in the Hat Song Book* (1967), *The Cat's Quizzer* (1976), and *I Can Read with My Eyes Shut!* (1978). The Cat has grown so popular that its creator now says cats follow him wherever he goes. The Cat has even been photographed in the library of Dartmouth College, barely visible inside a top hat that once belonged to Daniel Webster, and has been transformed into a giant ice sculpture for the 1981 Dartmouth Winter Carnival, in keeping with that year's theme, Hanover Hears a Who—A Tribute to Dr. Seuss.

By the 1960s Dr. Seuss had become an industry. *Green Eggs and Ham* (1960) was extremely successful; children still mail to him green eggs and ham as tokens of affection. Dr. Seuss characters were made into toys. In 1961 he

8 6
7
We looked!
Then
And we saw him step in on the mat!
We looked!
And we saw him!
The Cat in the Hat!
And he said to us,
"Why do you sit there like that?"
7
"I know it is wet
And the sun is not sunny.
But we can have
Lots of good fun that is funny!"

We looked! Then we saw him step in on the mat!, **working rough drawing from *The Cat in the Hat*, 1957 [127].**

We looked! Then we saw him step in on the mat! **from *The Cat in the Hat,* 1957 [128].**

wrote "What Was I Scared Of?," a very different type of story that may be his favorite. Published in *The Sneetches and Other Stories*, it centers on a hero who overcomes his nighttime fear of a "pair of pale green pants with nobody inside them." The Sneetch story is a lighthearted treatise on the ills of compulsive conformity, and "What Was I Scared Of?" combines an Ichabod Crane-like apparition with an almost mystical paean to self-reliance. In 1968 he launched yet another learn-to-read concept, and with the creation of *The Foot Book*, pioneered a new department at Random House, Bright & Early Books, for preschool and kindergarten readers.

The Lorax (1971), in Dr. Seuss's current opinion, is his best book. The title character, who also appears in the award-winning television special of 1972, is concerned with the effects of environmental pollution on his friends the Truffula Trees, the Brown Bar-ba Loots, the Humming Fish, and the Swomee Swans. Dr. Seuss enjoys telling this story about another Lorax fan:

> I don't have *The Lorax* here [at home]. It's in Texas, and you may wonder why. I was at a dinner for Democrats some years ago, and I sat next to Liz Carpenter, who was LBJ's press secretary. Since Lady Bird was so interested in beautification, it seemed that environmental protection was a safe topic, so I mentioned that I had written a book on the subject. Liz seemed interested, but soon after she left the room. When she reappeared she called me to the phone and

He was eating a cake in the tub!
from *The Cat in the Hat Comes Back*, 1958 [136].

And then he was gone with a tip of his hat
from *The Cat in the Hat*, 1957 [134].

Braille edition [135], *The Cat in the Hat Comes Back,* 1958.

C
B
A

Most people are scared to go on and beyond
from *On Beyond Zebra,* 1955 [115].

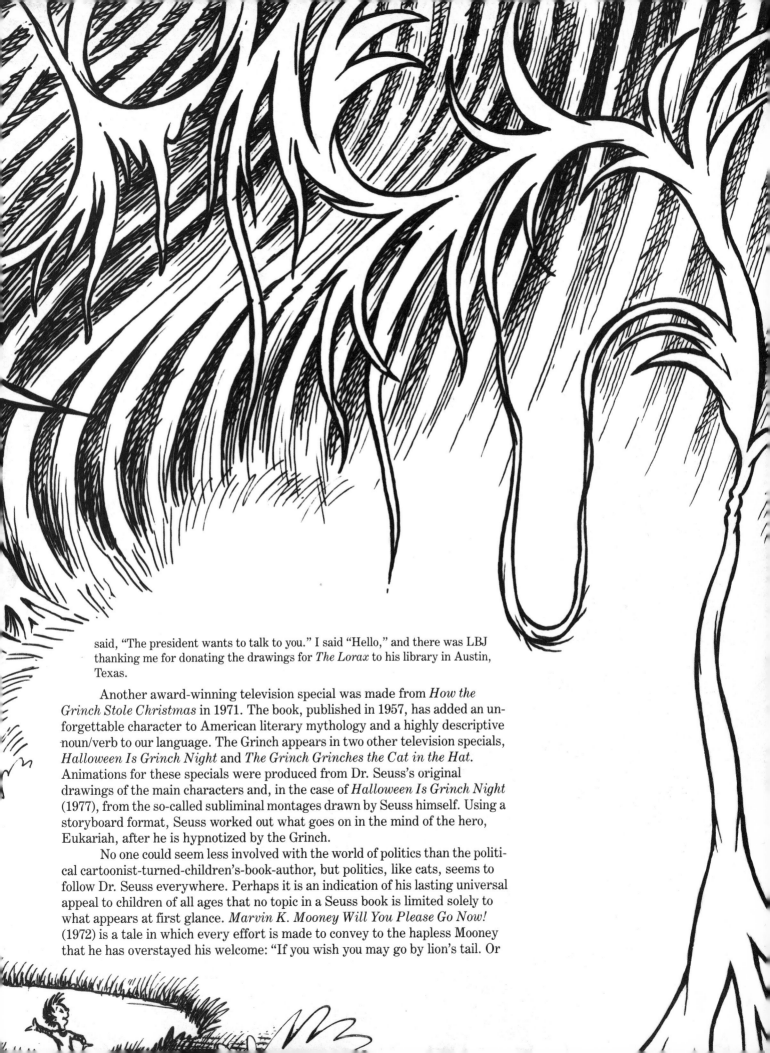

said, "The president wants to talk to you." I said "Hello," and there was LBJ thanking me for donating the drawings for *The Lorax* to his library in Austin, Texas.

Another award-winning television special was made from *How the Grinch Stole Christmas* in 1971. The book, published in 1957, has added an unforgettable character to American literary mythology and a highly descriptive noun/verb to our language. The Grinch appears in two other television specials, *Halloween Is Grinch Night* and *The Grinch Grinches the Cat in the Hat*. Animations for these specials were produced from Dr. Seuss's original drawings of the main characters and, in the case of *Halloween Is Grinch Night* (1977), from the so-called subliminal montages drawn by Seuss himself. Using a storyboard format, Seuss worked out what goes on in the mind of the hero, Eukariah, after he is hypnotized by the Grinch.

No one could seem less involved with the world of politics than the political cartoonist-turned-children's-book-author, but politics, like cats, seems to follow Dr. Seuss everywhere. Perhaps it is an indication of his lasting universal appeal to children of all ages that no topic in a Seuss book is limited solely to what appears at first glance. *Marvin K. Mooney Will You Please Go Now!* (1972) is a tale in which every effort is made to convey to the hapless Mooney that he has overstayed his welcome: "If you wish you may go by lion's tail. Or

Presentation copy, ***Happy Birthday to You!,*** 1959 [141]; cover, ***Green Eggs and Ham,*** 1960 [150].

HAPPY BIRTHDAY TO YOU!
BB
By
Dr. Seuss

Green Eggs and Ham
I CAN READ IT ALL BY MYSELF
Beginner Books
A 50 WORD BOOK
By Dr. Seuss

Look! Dr. Derring's Singing Herrings!
from *Happy Birthday to You!*, 1959 [145].

MERRY CHRISTMAS
WHO Express
FOR JO-JO
FOR UNCLE WHO

Then he slid down the chimney **from** ***How the Grinch Stole Christmas!*****, 1957 [125].**

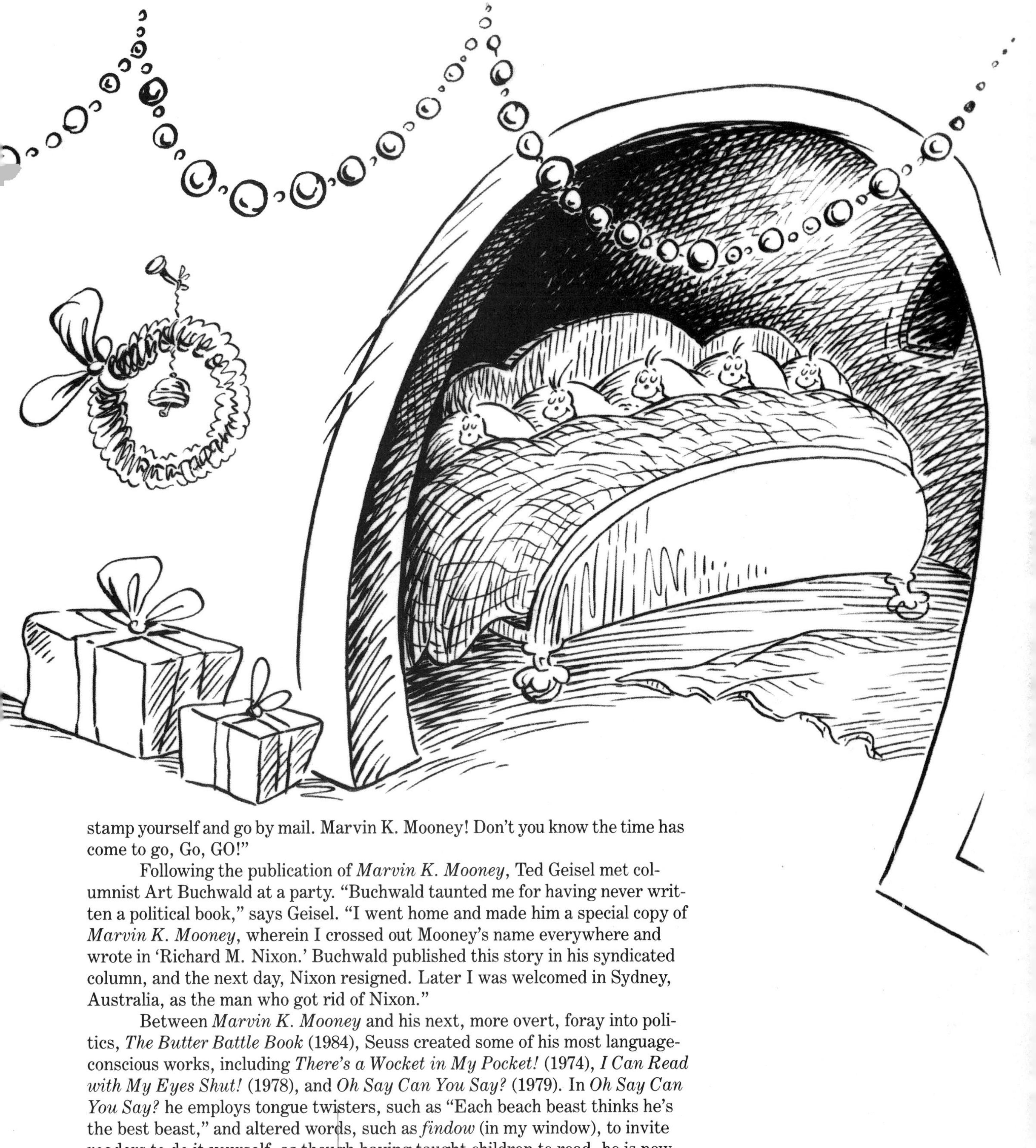

stamp yourself and go by mail. Marvin K. Mooney! Don't you know the time has come to go, Go, GO!"

Following the publication of *Marvin K. Mooney*, Ted Geisel met columnist Art Buchwald at a party. "Buchwald taunted me for having never written a political book," says Geisel. "I went home and made him a special copy of *Marvin K. Mooney*, wherein I crossed out Mooney's name everywhere and wrote in 'Richard M. Nixon.' Buchwald published this story in his syndicated column, and the next day, Nixon resigned. Later I was welcomed in Sydney, Australia, as the man who got rid of Nixon."

Between *Marvin K. Mooney* and his next, more overt, foray into politics, *The Butter Battle Book* (1984), Seuss created some of his most language-conscious works, including *There's a Wocket in My Pocket!* (1974), *I Can Read with My Eyes Shut!* (1978), and *Oh Say Can You Say?* (1979). In *Oh Say Can You Say?* he employs tongue twisters, such as "Each beach beast thinks he's the best beast," and altered words, such as *findow* (in my window), to invite readers to do it yourself, as though having taught children to read, he is now determined to inspire them to imagine and perhaps to write. In these works he has created an outstanding operational model for what can be accomplished with words.

Dr. Seuss's
SLEEP BOOK
Dr. Seuss's SLEEP BOOK
RANDOM HOUSE
red = 100
100 red
40 red
blue = 10

Cover, *Dr. Seuss's Sleep Book,* 1962 [161]; presentation copy, *How the Grinch Stole Christmas!,* 1957 [122].

How The
GRINCH
STOLE
CHRISTMAS!
By
Dr. Seuss

Ninety-nine zillion,
Nine trillion and two
Creatures are sleeping!
So...
How about you?

Ninety-nine zillion nine trillion and two creatures are sleeping! **from** ***Dr. Seuss's Sleep Book,*** **1962 [166].**

Everywhere, creatures
Are falling asleep.
The Collapsible Frink
Just collapsed in a heap.
And, by adding the Frink
To the others before,
I am able to give you
The Who's-Asleep-Score:
Right now, forty thousand
Four hundred and four
Creatures are happily,
Deeply in slumber.
I think you'll agree
That's a whopping fine number.

George's
Henry's
Freddy's
Way out in the west, in the town of Merced
The Hinkle-Horn Honking Club just went to bed.
Every horn has been quietly hung on a hook,
For the night, in its own private Hinkle-Horn Nook.
All this long, happy day, they've been honking about
And the Hinkle-Horn Honkers have honked themselves out.
But they'll wake up quite fresh in the morning. And then...
They'll start right in Hinkle-Horn honking again.
40

The Collapsible Frink just collapsed in a heap [163] and ***The Hinkle-Horn Honking Club just went to bed*** [162] from ***Dr. Seuss's Sleep Book***, 1962.

BIG R
little r
Rosy Robbin Ross.
Rosy's going riding
on her
red rhinoceros.

Red Hair and Tail
of Big Animal #2 Red.
Tongue & rest of Body Square
are #34.
Yellows: #17
Blue Sky #35
Blue Base #3
I am a
Zizzer-Zazzer-Zuzz
as you can
plainly see

Big R little r Rosy Robbin Ross **[167] and *I am a Zizzer Zazzer Zuzz*** **[168] from *Dr. Seuss's ABC*, 1963.**

Lettering #18
No outline
YAWN SONG
Face 17
teeth white
3 Double Staves
ON CAT'S BODY
BELOW NECKTIE.
Super impose 30% Gray Tone
Blue = #48
All mouths, tongues 40% Red

I CAN SING LOUDER than YOU
MODERATO
(FIRST VOICE) START VERY QUIET
I CAN SING LOUD - ER, LOUD-ER THAN YOU

Preliminary drawings, *The Cat in the Hat Song Book*, 1967 [177, 180].

I can lick twenty-two tigers today **from *I Can Lick 30 Tigers Today! and Other Stories*, 1969 [186].**

The words of Dr. Seuss made headlines in 1984, when *The Butter Battle Book* attracted the attention of Mario Cuomo, governor of New York. The story of an arms race between the Yooks, who eat their bread butter-side up, and the Zooks, who eat it butter-side down, *The Butter Battle Book* was described by Governor Cuomo as a "magnificent little volume," which he urged everyone to read for a clearer understanding of the issues surrounding nuclear war.[11] "It's a good title, too, don't you think?" asks Geisel. "Audrey said she would leave me if I gave it the title *I* wanted." Widowed in 1967, Dr. Seuss now shares his mountaintop home in La Jolla, California, with his second wife, Audrey Stone Geisel. Her opinions are very important to him, and she has a finely developed sixth sense about when to appear with a suggestion or tie-breaking vote.

In February 1985 Theodor Geisel appeared on stage at Radio City Music Hall along with the Rockettes and fellow honorees, including Lillian Gish, at the Actors Fund Night of One Hundred Stars. The previous year he was awarded the Pulitzer Prize, which reads: "Theodor Seuss Geisel, a Pulitzer Prize in Special Citation for his special contribution over nearly half a century to the education and enjoyment of America's children and their parents." Later in 1985 he received a doctor of fine arts from Princeton University. The citation is as follows:

> He makes house calls in the land of our first dreams and fears, where naughty cats wear hats, and the menace of the Grinch is real. From Mulberry Street to

The
LORAX
By
Dr. Seuss

Preliminary drawing for cover, *The Lorax,* 1971 [194].

THNEEDS
THNEEDS
YOU NEED A THNEED
NORTH
WEST
YOU NEED A THNEED
SOUTH
EAST
I meant no harm. I most truly did not.
But I had to grow bigger. So bigger I got.
I biggered my factory. I biggered my roads.
I biggered my wagons. I biggered the loads
of the Thneeds I shipped out. I was shipping them forth
to the South! To the East! To the West! To the North!
I went right on biggering... selling more Thneeds.
And I biggered my money, which everyone needs.
YOU NEED A THNEED

Spread and cover, *The Lorax*, 1971.

> Solla Sollew he leads us through the brightly colored landscape of imagination, a place of improbable rhymes and impossible names, odd creatures and curious food. Encouraging children to read beyond zebra, to count fishes red and blue, he gives them their first mastery over the mystery of signs. He shows them the way to the adult world, as he shows adults the way to the child.[12]

The
LORAX
By
Dr. Seuss

To his dismay, when he came forward to accept the degree, the audience began to recite *Green Eggs and Ham.*

A visit to Dr. Seuss's studio is an instructive experience. He works in his home atop Mount Soledad, reached only by a narrow, winding road that has been under repair "for about a year." The view is breathtaking and so are the curves, which could easily be found in the world of Seuss books. Some nearby trees are eucalyptus, while others are straight out of the pages of *Solla Sollew.* In fact, it's easy to imagine that everything in this remote world inspired a book; or the influence of the books is so pervasive that our perceptions of the real world are altered by them. "Good afternoon," says Dr. Seuss, appearing at the gate. "Don't trip over the cat. Its name is Thing One."

He is tall and his eyes twinkle, but he doesn't look like Santa Claus or your grandfather. He doesn't speak in rhyme. He wants to talk about his latest book *You're Only Old Once!* and strides past the swimming pool, through the house, and into the studio where a wall of windows faces north. On some days

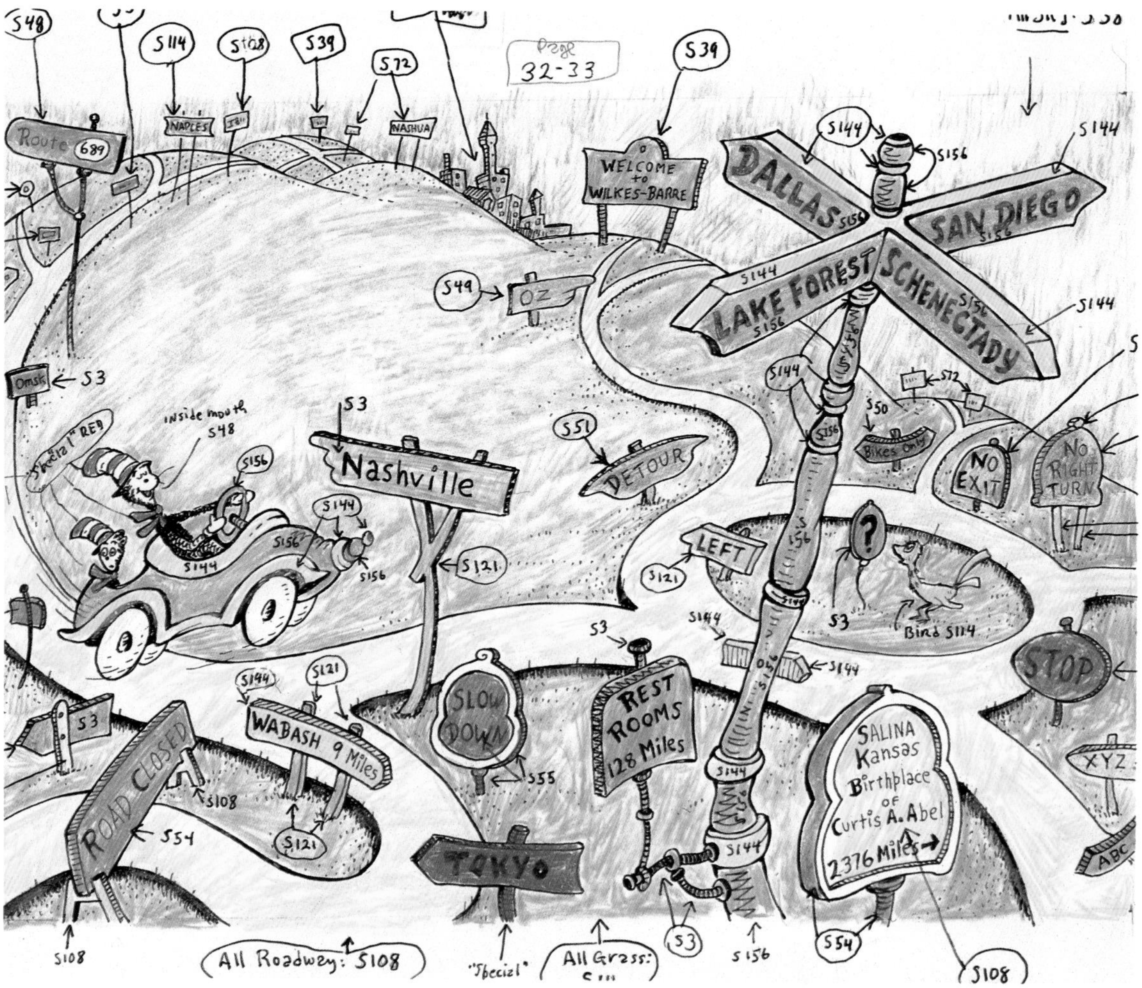
Page 32-33
Route 689
NAPLES
NASHUA
WELCOME to WILKES-BARRE
DALLAS
SAN DIEGO
LAKE FOREST
SCHENECTADY
OZ
Omsk
inside mouth S48
Nashville
DETOUR
Bikes Only
NO EXIT
NO RIGHT TURN
LEFT
Bird S114
STOP
SLOW DOWN
REST ROOMS 128 Miles
WABASH 9 Miles
ROAD CLOSED
TOKYO
SALINA Kansas Birthplace of Curtis A. Abel 2376 Miles
XYZ
ABC
All Roadway: S108
"Specizl"
All Grass:

I Can Read with my Eyes Shut!
By Dr. Seuss

The CAT'S QUIZZER
HOW? WHAT? WHO? WHY?
By Dr. Seuss

If you read with your eyes shut **[225] and preliminary drawing for cover [224] from *I Can Read with My Eyes Shut!*, 1978; cover [220], *The Cat's Quizzer*, 1976.**

Pages 6-7
Wood 40% Yellow
Cart 40% Blue
Horse collar 35
39 wheels and axels
Ropes 17
Note. All faces and hands are 53.
All eyes are white

Just suppose, for example, you lived in Ga-Zayt **from *Did I Ever Tell You How Lucky You Are?*, 1973 [206].**

he can see an island eighty-five miles out to sea; on others he sees only his patio through a fog bank. "This is where I wrote *You're Only Old Once!* See, the drawings are still on the wall." When questioned on whether he writes the story or makes the drawings first, he replies, "No rules."

You're Only Old Once! bears the legend "Is this a children's book? Well... not immediately. You buy a copy for your child now and you give it to him on his 70th birthday." On the dust jacket is the subtitle: *A Book for Obsolete Children.* At work on the book for nearly a year, Geisel is eager to describe how he did it. "People think you can just sit down and write a children's book in an afternoon but look at all this." He waved his hands toward more than twenty drawings on tracing paper tacked to the wall of his studio. These drawings, which he calls his working roughs, are in color. On many are pasted bits of handwritten or typed text. Each drawing represents a page in *You're Only Old Once!* He brings out a thick folder of papers with fragments of drawings, lists of words such as *psychomuftics*, *pharmabinomials*, *uncleology*, *gollogenetics*, and other odds and ends. "This is the bone pile, the thoughts that got nowhere." The bone pile contains enough rough drawings for another book, easily. "Do you know what happens next? I make these finished drawings with pen and ink. You're lucky. I just got everything back from my publisher in the mail today." The finished drawings are larger versions of the working roughs, but they don't

You can think about red **from** ***Oh, the Thinks You Can Think!*****, 1975 [218].**

In those green-pastured mountains
of Fotta-fa-Zee
everybody feels fine
at a hundred and three
'cause the air that they breath
is potassium-free
and because they chew nuts
from the Nunk-Funkler tree.
This gives strength to their teeth.
It gives length to their hair
and theylive without Doctors,
with nary a care.

Working rough drawing, ***You're Only Old Once!***, 1986 [243a].

Those Boys in the Back room sure knew how to putter!
They made me a thing called the Utterly Sputter
and I jumped aboard with my heart all a-flutter
and steered toward the land
of the Upside Down Butter.
My machine was so modern, so frightfully new
no one knew quite exactly just what it would do!
But it had several faucets that sprinkled Blue Goo
that, somehow, would splash on the Zooks as I flew
and gum up that upside-down butter they chew.

Hand-colored photostat, ***Those Boys in the Back Room sure knew how to putter!*** from ***The Butter Battle Book***, 1984 [237].

You're Only
Old Once!
By
Dr. Seuss
A Book for
Obsolete
Children

Cover, ***You're Only Old Once!*, 1986.**

resemble the brightly colored pages of the finished book. "Look at this. They make a black-and-white photostat, and I put the colors in by hand. Then I must number them all according to the color chart that Random House uses. Then they make these color proofs. I even choose the binding and the cover." He piles up catalogues and sample books and finished book covers for several editions of *You're Only Old Once!* "It takes more than an afternoon, hmmmmmmmmmm?"

It took more than an afternoon just to look at it all.

Mary Stofflet
Curator
San Diego Museum of Art

Dietician Von Eiffel controls the *Wuff-Whiffer,*
our Diet-Devising Computerized Sniffer,
on which you just simply lie down in repose
and sniff at good food as it goes past your nose.
From caviar soufflé to caribou roast,
from pemmican patties to terrapin toast,
he'll find out by Sniff-Scan the foods you like most.
And when that guy finds out
what you like,
you can bet it
won't be on your diet.
From here on, forget it!
COATS
SOCKS
PANTS

Proof, *You're Only Old Once!*, 1986 [247].

For your Pill Drill you'll go to Room Six Sixty-three,
where a voice will instruct you, "Repeat after me...
This small white pill is what I munch
at breakfast and right after lunch.
I take the pill that's kelly green
before each meal and in between.
These loganberry-colored pills
I take for early morning chills.
I take the pill with zebra stripes
to cure my early evening gripes.
These orange-tinted ones, of course,
I take to cure my charley horse.
"I take three blues at half past eight
to slow my exhalation rate.
On alternate nights at nine p.m.
I swallow pinkies. Four of them.
The reds, which make my eyebrows strong,
I eat like popcorn all day long.
The speckled browns are what I keep
beside my bed to help me sleep.
This long flat one is what I take
if I should die before I wake."
PILL DRILL

Spread from *You're Only Old Once!*, 1986.

NOTES

All direct quotations are from conversations between Theodor S. Geisel and the author, December 1985, January and February 1986, La Jolla, California.

1. Evelyn Waugh, *Vile Bodies* (Boston: Little, Brown and Co., 1930), 170–71.
2. Pamphlet, Theodor Geisel Papers, Department of Special Collections, University Research Library, University of California, Los Angeles.
3. Typescript, Geisel Papers.
4. Manuscript, Geisel Papers.
5. Typescript, Geisel Papers.
6. Typescript, Geisel Papers.
7. Bill Blackbeard and Martin Williams, eds., *The Smithsonian Collection of Newspaper Comics* (Washington, D.C., and New York: Smithsonian Institution Press and Harry N. Abrams, Inc., 1977), 287.
8. Pamphlet, Geisel Papers.
9. Typescript, Geisel Papers
10. John Hersey, "Why Do Students Bog Down on the First R?," *Life*, 24 May 1954, 136–37.
11. Michael Oreskes, "Civil Defense Planning Is Futile, Cuomo Says," *New York Times*, 15 May 1984, B1.
12. *Dartmouth Alumni Quarterly* (November 1985): 46.

Portrait of Theodor Seuss Geisel, Class of 1925, by Everett Raymond Kinstler, 1982, oil on canvas. Commissioned by Dartmouth College, Hanover, N.H.

Chronology

1904 Theodor Seuss Geisel born March 2 in Springfield, Massachusetts.

1922–25 Attends Dartmouth College, Hanover, New Hampshire.

1925 Is editor-in-chief of Dartmouth's humor magazine, *Jack-o-Lantern.* Graduates from Dartmouth.

1925–26 Attends Lincoln College, Oxford, England.

1926–27 Travels through Europe.

1927 Returns to United States. Lives in New York until 1943.

Sells first cartoons to *Judge* magazine. Publishes steady stream of cartoons and prose for *College Humor, Liberty, Vanity Fair,* and *Life.*

Creates "Quick, Henry, the Flit!" advertising campaign.

1931 Illustrates *Boners* for Viking Press.

Theodor S. Geisel, Springfield (Mass.) Central High School, c. 1921.

Oxford, England, 1926. Theodor S. Geisel, ***fourth row up, sixth from right.***

Ice sculpture made by Theodor S. Geisel, Phi Gam House, Dartmouth Winter Carnival, 1930–31.

With Guy Lombardo, *right,* examining a diploma for the Seuss Navy, Essomarine advertising campaign, c. 1936. The Seuss Navy was the largest in the world at the time.

At work in his studio, c. 1940.

Army Signal Corps, c. 1944. Theodor S. Geisel, *second from right,* Meredith Willson, *seated.*

1935 Creates Essomarine advertising campaign for Standard Oil Company of New Jersey.

Creates the cartoon strip *Hejji* for Hearst newspapers.

1937 Writes his first book for children, *And to Think That I Saw It on Mulberry Street.*

1938 *The 500 Hats of Bartholomew Cubbins* is published.

1939 *The King's Stilts* is published.

The Seven Lady Godivas, a book for adults, is published.

1940 *Horton Hatches the Egg* is published.

1940–42 Works as editorial cartoonist for *PM* newspaper.

1943–46 Serves in Army Signal Corps during World War II. Receives Legion of Merit for educational and informational films.

1946 Academy Award, Best Documentary Short Subject, for *Hitler Lives,* written for the army as *Your Job in Germany.*

Moves permanently to California.

1947 Academy Award, Best Documentary Feature, for *Design for Death,* a history of the Japanese people, written in collaboration with Helen Palmer Geisel.

McElligot's Pool is published.

1948 Moves to La Jolla, California.

Thidwick the Big-Hearted Moose is published.

1949 Creates advertising campaign for Ford.

Bartholomew and the Oobleck is published.

1950 *If I Ran the Zoo* is published.

1951 Academy Award, Animated Cartoon, for *Gerald McBoing-Boing.*

1952 Writes and designs *The 5000 Fingers of Dr. T.,* a full-length feature film.

With the cast from the movie *The 5000 Fingers of Dr. T.,* 1951.

With the Cat in the Hat, 1960s.

Theodor and Audrey Geisel on Cat in the Hat float, Thanksgiving Day parade, Detroit, November 1979.

Dr.
Seuss

Cats follow him wherever he goes.

The Cat in the Hat in a classroom, Denver, February 1976.

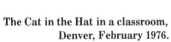

The Cat in the Hat in Daniel Webster's top hat, Library, Dartmouth College, June 1975.

1953 *Scrambled Eggs Super!* is published.

1954 Writes "Modern Art on Horseback," script for a television-radio workshop sponsored by the Ford Foundation and aired on NBC. Actors include Hans Conried, Burgess Meredith, Dr. Seuss.

Horton Hears a Who! is published.

1954–56 Creates advertising campaign for Holly Sugar.

1955 *On Beyond Zebra!* is published.

1956 Receives doctor of humane letters (hon.) from Dartmouth. Creates *Signs of Civilization*, anti-billboard pamphlet, for the city of La Jolla.

If I Ran the Circus is published.

1957 *How the Grinch Stole Christmas!* and *The Cat in the Hat* are published.

1958 Becomes president of Beginner Books, a division of Random House, Inc.

Exhibits at the Fine Arts Gallery, San Diego.

The Cat in the Hat Comes Back and *Yertle the Turtle and Other Stories* are published.

1959 *Happy Birthday to You!* is published.

1960 *One Fish Two Fish Red Fish Blue Fish* and *Green Eggs and Ham* are published.

1961 *The Sneetches and Other Stories* is published.

1962 *Dr. Seuss's Sleep Book* is published.

1962 *Dr. Seuss's ABC* and *Hop on Pop* are published.

1965 *Fox in Socks* and *I Had Trouble in Getting to Solla Sollew* are published.

1967 *The Cat in the Hat Song Book* is published.

1968 Receives doctor of humane letters (hon.) from American International College, Springfield, Massachusetts.

The Foot Book is published.

Schoolchildren in the Cat's striped hats. From a photograph album sent to Theodor S. Geisel from Woodridge, Ill., 1982.

Dr. Seuss

The Cat in the Hat ice sculpture, Dartmouth Winter Carnival, 1981.

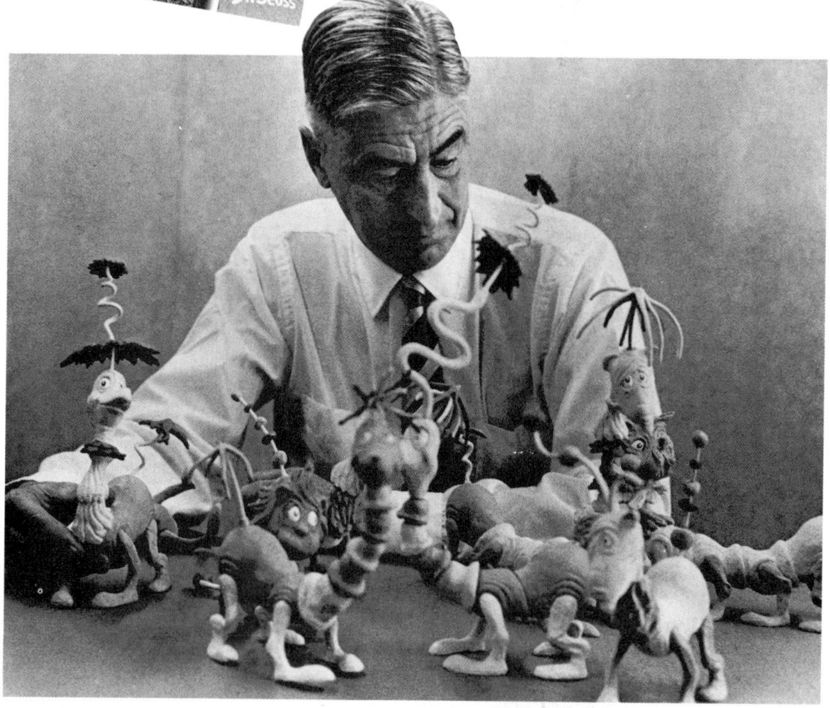

With models for toys based on his characters, 1959.

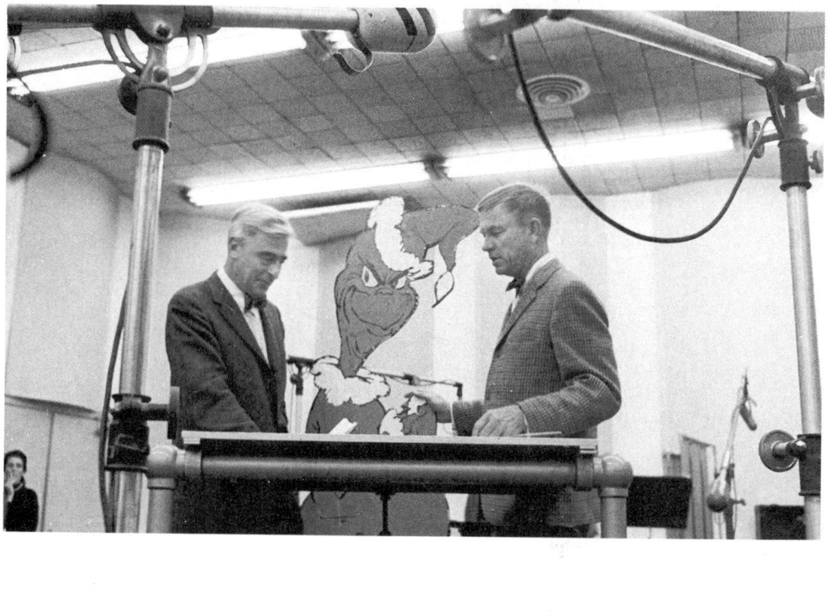

With Chuck Jones, *right,* producer, recording *How the Grinch Stole Christmas* television special, 1970.

1969 *I Can Lick 30 Tigers Today! and Other Stories* and *My Book about Me* are published.

1970 *I Can Draw It Myself* and *Mr. Brown Can Moo! Can You?* are published.

1971 Receives Peabody Awards for television specials *How the Grinch Stole Christmas* and *Horton Hears a Who.*

The Lorax is published.

1972 Receives Critics Award, International Animated Cartoon Festival, Zagreb, Yugoslavia, and Silver Medal, International Film and TV Festival of New York for *The Lorax.*

Marvin K. Mooney Will You Please Go Now! is published.

1973 *Did I Ever Tell You How Lucky You Are?* and *The Shape of Me and Other Stuff* are published.

1974 *There's a Wocket in My Pocket!* and *Great Day for Up!* are published.

1975 *Fiftieth Anniversary Retrospective* is organized by Dartmouth.

Oh, the Thinks You Can Think! is published.

With Robert Bernstein, *right,* president of Random House, 1977.

With Blue-Green Abelard, c. 1982.

1976 Receives first Outstanding California Author Award from California Association of Teachers of English.

The Cat's Quizzer is published.

1976–77 Exhibits at La Jolla Museum of Contemporary Art.

1977 Receives doctor of humane letters (hon.) from Lake Forest College, Illinois.

Receives Emmy Award, Best Children's Special, for *Halloween Is Grinch Night.*

1978 Receives Roger Revelle Award from University of California, San Diego.

I Can Read with My Eyes Shut! is published.

1979 *Oh Say Can You Say?* is published.

With E. L. Doctorow, *right*, c. 1980.

With Maurice Sendak, *right*, San Diego Museum of Art, 1983.

Lion wading pool, Wild Animal Park, San Diego, donated by Theodor S. Geisel, c. 1973. Geisel considers this his greatest work.

1980 Receives doctor of literature (hon.) from Whittier College, California.

Receives Laura Ingalls Wilder Award from Association for Library Service to Children, American Library Association.

1981 Dr. Seuss Day is proclaimed by governors of Alabama, Arkansas, California, Delaware, Georgia, Kansas, Minnesota, and Utah to celebrate Seuss's seventy-seventh birthday.

1982 Receives Regina Medal from Catholic Library Association.

Receives Special Award for Distinguished Service to Children from National Association of Elementary School Principals.

Receives Emmy Award, Best Children's Special, for *The Grinch Grinches the Cat in the Hat.*

Hunches in Bunches is published.

1983 Receives doctor of literature (hon.) from J. F. Kennedy University, Orinda, California.

1984 Receives Pulitzer Prize.

The Butter Battle Book is published.

1985 Receives doctor of fine arts (hon.) from Princeton University, New Jersey.

1986 *You're Only Old Once!* is published.

Dr. Seuss

Random House warehouse, Westminister, Md., with Dr. Seuss flag, which is flown while books are being shipped out, 1975.

Checklist

All works are from the collection of the Department of Special Collections, University Research Library, University of California, Los Angeles, unless otherwise noted. All drawings are by Theodor S. Geisel. Measurements are in inches, height preceding width; all works are on paper unless otherwise noted. A bullet (•) indicates that a work is illustrated.

Early Work

Jack-o-Lantern

• 1. Financial Note: *Goat Milk is Higher than Ever*, 1925
reproduction, 8 5/8 x 9 3/4 in.

2. *Dr. Seuss' Poetry Corner: Pentellic Bilge for Valentine's Birthday*, 1936
reproduction, 12 x 8 3/4 in.

• 3. Notebook of Theodor S. Geisel, Lincoln College, Oxford University, 1925–26
pencil and ink with metal and binding fabric, 9 5/8 x 6 5/8 in.
Collection of Theodor S. Geisel

Roman and Florentine Period

• 4a. *Romulus and Remus*, c. 1925–27
ink, 8 x 10 5/8 in.
Collection of Theodor S. Geisel

4b. *Scene on the Forum with Vestal Virgins*, c. 1925–27
pencil, ink, and crayon, 8 1/4 x 10 3/4 in.
Collection of Theodor S. Geisel

• 4c. *Dragon*, after a painting by Piero di Cosimo in the Uffizi Gallery, Florence, c. 1925–27
pencil, ink, and crayon, 7 3/4 x 10 3/4 in.
Collection of Theodor S. Geisel

Judge

• 5a. *Jungle Number*, cover, 1929
reproduction, 11 1/8 x 8 1/2 in.

• 5b. Cover, 1933
reproduction, 11 1/2 x 8 1/2 in.

• 5c. *Technocracy Number*, cover, 1933
reproduction, 11 1/2 x 8 1/2 in.

6. *How many times must I tell you, Kiwi*, c. 1930s
reproduction, 11 5/16 x 8 1/2 in.

7. *Symphonix*, 1932
negative stat, 10 3/16 x 15 7/8 in.
Collection of Theodor S. Geisel

8. *Boners and More Boners*, advertisement, 1931
reproduction, 11 1/2 x 2 7/8 in.

9. *Boners*, 1931
book, 6 1/4 x 5 1/8 in.
Collection of Theodor S. Geisel

10. *More Boners*, 1931
book, 6 1/4 x 5 1/4 in.
Collection of Theodor S. Geisel

11. *The Pocket Book of Boners*, 1961
book, 6 3/8 x 4 1/4 in.
Collection of Theodor S. Geisel

Liberty

12. *Goofy Olympics*, 1932
reproduction, 11 1/2 x 8 1/2 in.

University

13. *Some Mooses I Have Known*, 1933
reproduction, 11 11/16 x 8 5/16 in.

Life

• 14. *I know, my dear, but that's* NOTHING *compared to having an egg!*, c. 1929–30
reproduction, 11 11/16 x 8 3/4 in.

15a. *The Changing Fauna of the Arctic; Some Recent Developments in Adaptation*, c. 1929–30
reproduction, 11 9/16 x 8 11/16 in.

• 15b. *We're lost if we steer by the Great North Bear; steer by the Small South Whoosis!*, c. 1929–30
reproduction, 11 3/4 x 8 3/4 in.

The Advertising Business at a Glance

16a. *The Account Executive*, c. 1930–35
watercolor, 13 x 17 in.
Collection of Theodor S. Geisel

16b. *"Now Let's Really Analyze that Humorous Advertising,"* c. 1930–35
watercolor, 13 x 17 in.
Collection of Theodor S. Geisel

16c. *The Man with an Idea*, c. 1930–35
watercolor, 13 x 17 in.
Collection of Theodor S. Geisel

College Humor

17a. *Animals Every Student Loves* by Doctor Theodophilus Seuss, Ph.D., I.Q., H_2SO_4, c. 1929–30
reproduction, 11 1/4 x 8 1/2 in.

17b. *Animals Every Student Loves* by Doctor Theodophilus Seuss, Ph.D., I.Q., S.O.L., c. 1929–30
reproduction, 11 1/4 x 8 1/2 in.

• 17c. *Animals Every Student Loves* by Dr. Theodophilus Seuss, Ph.D., I.Q., H_2SO_4, c. 1929–30
reproduction, 11¼ x 8½ in.

Hejji

• 18a. *Hejji*, Sunday, April 7, 1935
color proof, 17¼ x 11$^{15}/_{16}$ in.
Collection of Theodor S. Geisel

18b. *Hejji*, Sunday, April 14, 1935
color proof, 17¼ x 11$^{15}/_{16}$ in.
Collection of Theodor S. Geisel

18c. *Hejji*, Sunday, April 21, 1935
color proof, 17¼ x 11$^{15}/_{16}$ in.
Collection of Theodor S. Geisel

The New York Woman

19. *See Dr. Seuss For Social Publicity*, 1936
reproduction, 14$^{3}/_{16}$ x 9¾ in.

Calendar Art

20a. *Right nice August we're having, neighbor*, c. 1930s
reproduction, 4$^{11}/_{16}$ x 3 in.
Collection of Theodor S. Geisel

20b. *After All Reindeer are so Darned Common*, c. 1930s
reproduction, 4¾ x 3 in.
Collection of Theodor Geisel

• 20c. *Financial Note—Goat's Milk is Higher than Ever*, c. 1930s
reproduction, 4⅝ x 3 in.
Collection of Theodor S. Geisel

20d. *Well if it isn't William Osborn Esterhazy! Why, I knew you when you were* that *high!*, c. 1930s
reproduction, 5 x 3½ in.
Collection of Theodor S. Geisel

20e. *Bring on Your Dragons!*, c. 1930s
reproduction, 5 x 3½ in.
Collection of Theodor S. Geisel

20f. *F'gosh sakes, Julius . . . untwine, untwine!*, c. 1930s
reproduction, 5 x 3½ in.
Collection of Theodor S. Geisel

21. *On the Steppes of Russia*, illustration for poem done while shaving, c. 1938–39
pencil and ink, 13$^{15}/_{16}$ x 11$^{1}/_{16}$ in.
Collection of Theodor S. Geisel

Flit Advertising Campaign

22. *Flit Cartoons As They Have Appeared in Magazines throughout the Country*, 1929
booklet, 6$^{1}/_{16}$ x 5½ in.

23. *Quick, Henry, the Flit!*, 1930
reproduction, 11⅛ x 8¾ in.

24. *Flit Cartoons As They Have Appeared in Magazines throughout the Country*, 1930
booklet, 3$^{3}/_{16}$ x 8½ in.

25. Advertisement, c. 1930s
black-and-white proof, 11 x 8½ in.

26a. *Quick, Henry, the Flit!*, 1930
poster, 11 x 21 in.

• 26b. *Quick, Henry, the Flit!*, 1930
poster, 11 x 21 in.

27. *Don't Duck! Make Insects Detour!*, 1931
brochure, 5⅞ x 9$^{7}/_{16}$ in.

• 28a. *An Ancient News Picture*, n.d.
reproduction, 4$^{15}/_{16}$ x 4$^{11}/_{16}$ in.

28b. *Kelly Deep Sea Diving Co.*, n.d.
reproduction, 4$^{5}/_{16}$ x 5$^{9}/_{16}$ in.

28c. *Quick, Henry, the Flit!*, n.d.
reproduction, 3$^{13}/_{16}$ x 4$^{5}/_{16}$ in.

28d. *Schmucker and Flibb the Human Horse*, 1931
reproduction, 4$^{7}/_{16}$ x 5⅜ in.

28e. Advertisement, 1931
reproduction, 3$^{15}/_{16}$ x 4$^{13}/_{16}$ in.

28f. *Death to All Insects*, n.d.
reproduction, 3½ x 5⅜ in.

• 29. *Another Big Flit Year!*, 1931
booklet, 13 x 22 in.

30. *Adventures with a Flit Gun: A Collection of Flit Cartoons by Dr. Seuss*, 1932
booklet, 4¾ x 5⅞ in.

31. *Flit Kills Insects Quicker*, 1933
booklet, 13¾ x 10¾ in.

• 32. *Quick, Henry, the Flit!*, 1941
poster, 11 x 21 in.

33. Advertisement, 1949
proof sheet, 8⅛ x 6⅝ in.

NBC Radio Advertising Campaign

34. *The Statue of Liberty Comes in Third!*, c. 1931
brochure, 11 x 8½ in.
Collection of Theodor S. Geisel

35. *Everything's East at 7 A.M.*, c. 1931
brochure, 11 x 8½ in.
Collection of Theodor S. Geisel

36. *And What Makes* His *Particular Spots So Attractive?*, c. 1931
brochure, 12⅛ x 18$^{9}/_{16}$ in.
Collection of Theodor S. Geisel

37. *Here Are 4 Million Early Bird Families*, c. 1931
brochure, 14$^{1}/_{16}$ x 20$^{15}/_{16}$ in.
Collection of Theodor S. Geisel

Standard Oil Company of New Jersey Advertising Campaign

38. *Meet the Boys*, 1932
poster, 8 x 18 in.

39a. *Foil the Zero-doccus!*, 1932
poster, 11 x 21¼ in.

• 39b. *Foil the Karbo-nockus!*, 1933
poster, 11 x 21¼ in.

• 39c. *Foil the Moto-raspus!*, 1933
poster, 11 x 21 in.

40. *Secrets of the Deep*, 1935
pencil and ink, 7$^{7}/_{16}$ x 9$^{15}/_{16}$ in.
Collection of Theodor S. Geisel

41a. *Secrets of the Deep or the Perfect Yachtsman by Old Captain Taylor*, 1935
booklet, 9 x 6 in.

41b. *Secrets of the Deep, Vol. II by Old Captain Taylor, Aquatints by Dr. Seuss*, 1936
booklet, 9 x 6 in.

42. *Speaking of Portraits . . . Here's the Masterpiece in Oils!*, n.d.
color proof, 10⅞ x 8⅜ in.

• 43. *Seuss Navy Flag*, c. 1936
fabric with metal grommets, 16 x 24½ in.
Collection of Theodor S. Geisel

44. *Seuss Navy Diploma*, c. 1936
reproduction, 8½ x 9½ in.
Collection of Theodor S. Geisel

• 45. *Foiled by Essolube, a jig-saw melodrama*, c. 1930s
cardboard and paper, 17 x $11\frac{3}{4}$ in.
Collection of Theodor S. Geisel

46. *Essomarine Presents Little Dramas of the Deep*, 1938
brochure, $10\frac{7}{8}$ x $8\frac{7}{8}$ in.

_PM_ (newspaper)

• 47a. *Time to Get Up and Face the New Day!*, 1942
pencil and ink with typeset copy, $12\frac{5}{8}$ x $14\frac{11}{16}$ in.

47b. *Time to Get Up and Face the New Day!*, February 24, 1942
reproduction, $6\frac{7}{8}$ x $7\frac{11}{16}$ in.

• 48a. *And protect my beddie from the Communist Boogey Man!*, 1942
pencil and ink with typeset copy, $11\frac{7}{8}$ x $13\frac{1}{2}$ in.

48b. *And protect my beddie from the Communist Boogey Man!*, June 2, 1942
reproduction, $7\frac{7}{16}$ x $7\frac{5}{8}$ in.

• 49a. *The Alibi Boys: That Favorite Song and Dance Team of the Democratic Nations*, 1942
pencil and ink with typeset copy, $12\frac{5}{16}$ x $14\frac{1}{2}$ in.

49b. *The Alibi Boys*, July 14, 1942
reproduction, $7\frac{1}{4}$ x $8\frac{15}{16}$ in.

50a. *How to Bubble the Baby*, 1942
pencil and ink with typeset copy, $12\frac{3}{16}$ x 14 in.

50b. *How to Bubble the Baby*, July 23, 1942
reproduction, $6\frac{3}{4}$ x $7\frac{3}{4}$ in.

51a. *You see it's like this*, 1942
pencil and ink with typeset copy, $12\frac{7}{16}$ x $14\frac{3}{8}$ in.

51b. *You see it's like this*, September 25, 1942
reproduction, $6\frac{9}{16}$ x $7\frac{13}{16}$ in.

52a. *Scrap for Victory*, 1942
pencil and ink with typeset copy, $12\frac{1}{2}$ x $14\frac{3}{16}$ in.

52b. *Scrap for Victory*, October 1, 1942
reproduction, $6\frac{15}{16}$ x $7\frac{7}{8}$ in.

53a. *He's still strong on the Luft . . . but where's the Waffe?*, 1942
pencil and ink with typeset copy, $12\frac{5}{16}$ x $14\frac{1}{4}$ in.

53b. *He's still strong on the Luft . . . but where's the Waffe?*, December 1, 1942
reproduction, $6\frac{7}{8}$ x $7\frac{7}{8}$ in.

54. *You Can't Build a Substantial V Out of Turtles!*, March 20, 1942
reproduction, $6\frac{11}{16}$ x $7\frac{13}{16}$ in.

• 55. *Dr. Seuss, I Presume*, c. 1942
brochure, $8\frac{7}{8}$ x $5\frac{7}{8}$ in.

56. *Society of Red Tape Cutters Elects Roosevelt*, n.d.
reproduction, $13\frac{1}{16}$ x $10\frac{3}{16}$ in.

Ford Advertising Campaign

57. *They're Funny, They're Fast!*, 1949
brochure, 11 x $8\frac{1}{2}$ in.
Collection of Theodor S. Geisel

58. *Yes, you save with real Ford Service*, c. 1940s
brochure, $13\frac{3}{8}$ x $10\frac{1}{16}$ in.
Collection of Theodor S. Geisel

Holly Sugar Advertising Campaign

59a. *All it needs is . . . Holly Sugar*, 1954
poster, $9\frac{3}{8}$ x $20\frac{3}{8}$ in.

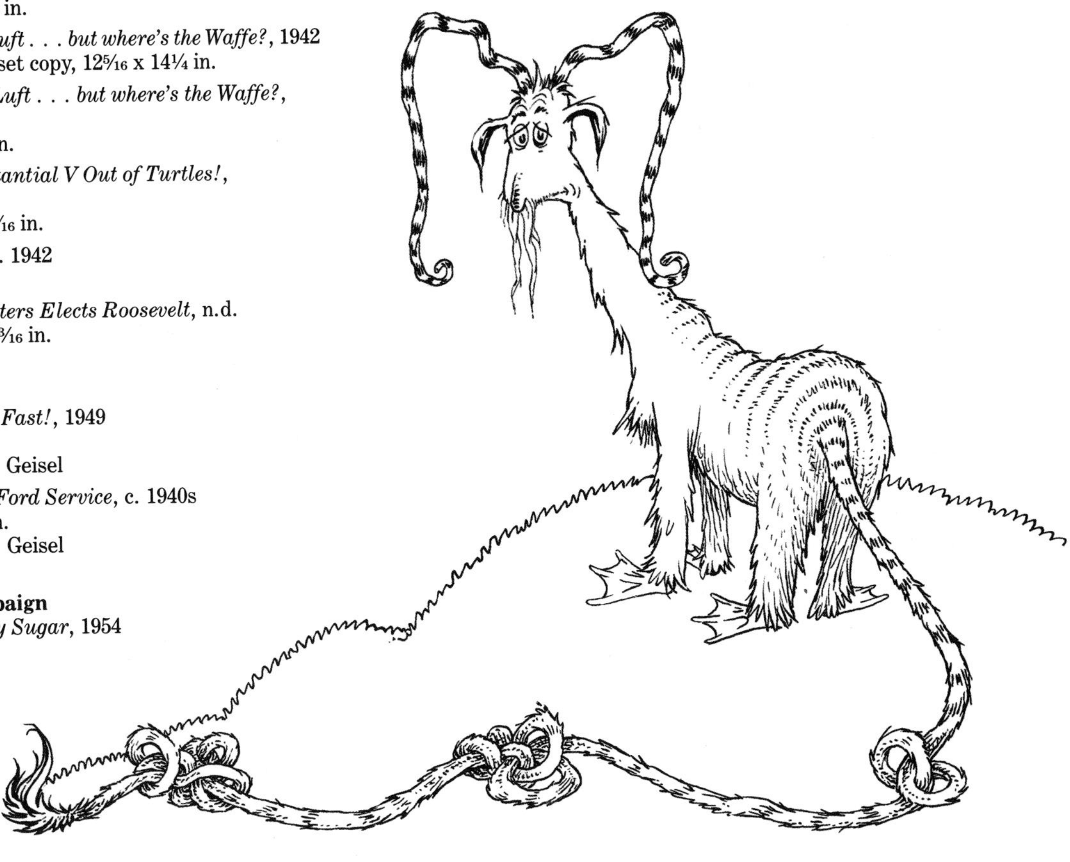

59b. *All they need is . . . Holly Sugar*, c. 1950s
poster, 9⅜ x 20⅜ in.

60. *Signs of Civilization*, 1956
pamphlet, 9 x 6 in.

Film and Television Animation

61. *Enter a Carefree Ormie in Festive Mood*, Ford television-commercial script, 1949
pencil and crayon, 11½ x 9¼ in.

The 5000 Fingers of Dr. T.

62a. *Dr. Terwilliger Costume for the Great Concert*, 1952
pencil, 11 x 8½ in.

62b. *Boy at Piano*, 1952
pencil, 11 x 8½ in.

62c. *Motor Pool*, 1952
pencil and watercolor, 8½ x 11 in.

• 62d. *Welcome*, 1952
pencil and watercolor, 8½ x 11 in.

How the Grinch Stole Christmas

63. Model sheet for television animation by Chuck Jones, 1971
color overlay on acetate and paper, 12½ x 10½ in.
Collection of Theodor S. Geisel

Pontoffel Pock, Where Are You

64a. Design for television film, 1979
crayon, 11 x 14 in.
Collection of Theodor S. Geisel

64b. Design for television film, 1979
pencil and crayon, 10½ x 12½ in.
Collection of Theodor S. Geisel

The Lorax

65. Model sheet for television animation by Chuck Jones, 1972
color overlay on acetate and paper, 14⁹⁄₁₆ x 16½ in.
Collection of Theodor S. Geisel

Karavan to Kubu

66a. Design for unproduced television film, c. 1975
pencil and crayon, 9 x 12 in.
Collection of Theodor S. Geisel

66b. Design for unproduced television film, c. 1975
pencil and crayon, 9¾ x 12½ in.
Collection of Theodor S. Geisel

66c. Design for unproduced television film, c. 1975
pencil and crayon, 11¹⁄₁₆ x 14 in.
Collection of Theodor S. Geisel

Halloween Is Grinch Night

67a. Montage for television animation, 1977
pencil and crayon, 8½ x 11 in.
Collection of Theodor S. Geisel

67b. Montage for television animation, 1977
pencil and crayon, 8⁹⁄₁₆ x 11¹⁄₁₆ in.
Collection of Theodor S. Geisel

67c. Montage for television animation, 1977
pencil and crayon, 5⅜ x 11 in.
Collection of Theodor S. Geisel

67d. Montage for television animation, 1977
pencil and crayon, 8½ x 14 in.
Collection of Theodor S. Geisel

67e. Montage for television animation, 1977
pencil and crayon, 8½ x 14 in.
Collection of Theodor S. Geisel

Paintings and Drawings

68. *Every Girl Should Have a Unicorn*, 1965
oil on board, 30 x 24 in.
Collection of Theodor S. Geisel

69. *Cat Detective Collecting Evidence in a Bad Part of Town*, 1969
watercolor on board, 20 x 15 in.
Collection of Theodor S. Geisel

70. *View from a Window of a Rented Beach Cottage*, n.d.
oil on board with hinged window frame and screen, 18½ x 23½ in.
Collection of Theodor S. Geisel

71. *Retired Thunderbird*, c. 1975
ink and crayon, 14¾ x 11⅞ in.
Collection of Theodor S. Geisel

72. *Impractical Marshmallow-Toasting Device*, c. 1975
ink and crayon, 12⅛ x 17¾ in.
Collection of Theodor S. Geisel

73. *O Sole Meow*, n.d.
oil on board, 23½ x 19⅜ in.
Collection of Theodor S. Geisel

74. *Cat Carnival in West Venice*, n.d.
watercolor on board, 12¾ x 13⅛ in.
Collection of Theodor S. Geisel

75. *The Stag at Eve*, n.d.
watercolor on board, 18³⁄₁₆ x 12⁵⁄₁₆ in.
Collection of Theodor S. Geisel

Books

***And to Think That I Saw It on Mulberry Street* (1937)**

76. Presentation copy, 1937
10⅞ x 8⅝ in.

77a. "These are the first words I ever wrote in the field of writing for children," 1963
typescript, 10½ x 7¼ in.

77b. Notes, 1936
holograph copy, 7¹⁄₁₆ x 5⁹⁄₁₆ in.

***The Seven Lady Godivas* (1939)**

• 78. *Lulu Godiva, after being kicked by her horse, records her Horse Truth in the book and leaves the place forever*, 1939
ink, watercolor, and crayon on board, 15⁹⁄₁₆ x 21⅝ in.

***The 500 Hats of Bartholomew Cubbins* (1938)**

• 79. Presentation copy, 1938
12⅛ x 9¼ in.

• 80. Japanese edition, 1949
10⅜ x 7¼ in.

81. Japanese edition, 1981
12 x 9½ in.
Collection of Theodor S. Geisel

82. Drawing for dust jacket, 1938
ink, watercolor, and crayon on board, 14³⁄₁₆ x 21⅞ in.

83. *Through the side window of the carriage, the King himself was staring back—straight back at him!*, 1938
crayon, 21⁹⁄₁₆ x 18⁵⁄₁₆ in.

84. *The Father of the Father of Nadd*, 1938
watercolor and crayon, 12⅝ x 9⁹⁄₁₆ in.

85. *The Yeoman of Bowmen*, 1938
watercolor and crayon, 14¾ x 13½ in.

86. *The magicians huddled over Bartholomew and chanted*, 1938
watercolor and crayon, 17 x 14⅛ in.

- 87. *He was wearing the most beautiful hat that had ever been seen in the Kingdom of Didd*, 1938
watercolor and crayon, 13 x 17⅜ in.

***The King's Stilts* (1939)**

88. Untitled, 1939
watercolor and crayon on board, 18⅞ x 16 in.

89. *With his left hand he could bathe with his royal bath brush, but his right he always had to keep dry for signing important papers of state*, 1939
watercolor and crayon on board, 15⅜ x 12⁹⁄₁₆ in.

90. *These Nizzards were always flying about over the Dike Trees, waiting for a chance to swoop down and peck*, 1939
watercolor and crayon on board, 14½ x 24 in.

***Horton Hatches the Egg* (1940)**

- 91. Dust jacket proof, 1940
10½ x 8⅝ in.

92. Braille edition, transcribed by Gladys Daniel, illustrated by John S. Lewinson, Brooklyn Industrial Home for the Blind, 1960
fabric, wood, plastic on paper, plastic spiral binding, 11 x 9¹⁵⁄₁₆ in.

- 93. *I'll sit on your egg and I'll try not to break it*, 1940
crayon, 13 x 10 in.

- 94. *They laughed and they laughed. Then they all ran away*, 1940
crayon, 13 x 18⁹⁄₁₆ in.

***McElligot's Pool* (1947)**

- 95. Drawing for dust jacket, 1947
pencil, ink, and watercolor with typeset copy on board, 15¹¹⁄₁₆ x 22¾ in.

96. Drawing for endpapers, 1947
watercolor on board, 12¾ x 18⅞ in.

97. *If I wait long enough, if I'm patient and cool, who knows what I'll catch in McElligot's Pool*, 1947
pencil and watercolor with typeset copy on board, 15 x 20¹⁵⁄₁₆ in.
Collection of Theodor S. Geisel

- 98. *The kind that likes flowers*, 1947
pencil and watercolor on board, 15³⁄₁₆ x 21³⁄₁₆ in.
Collection of Theodor S. Geisel

***Thidwick the Big-Hearted Moose* (1948)**

- 99. Presentation copy, 1948
11¹⁄₁₆ x 8⁷⁄₁₆ in.

100. Drawing for dust jacket, 1948
pencil, watercolor, and crayon on board, 13½ x 19¹⁄₁₆ in.

101. *Up at Lake Winna-Bango, one day, they were lunching*, 1948
pencil, watercolor, and crayon with typescript on board, 13 x 18½ in.

***Bartholomew and the Oobleck* (1949)**

102. Mock-up of book, 1949
pencil and crayon with typescript on paper and board, 12¼ x 9⅛ in.

103. *Came the magicians on their padded, shuffling feet*, 1949
pencil and watercolor, 12½ x 10¼ in.
Collection of Theodor S. Geisel

104. *He saw the Royal Fiddlers. They were stuck to their royal fiddles!*, 1949
pencil and crayon, 14⁵⁄₁₆ x 22 in.

- 105. *It was in the throne room that Bartholomew found him*, 1949
pencil and crayon, 14⅛ x 22 in.

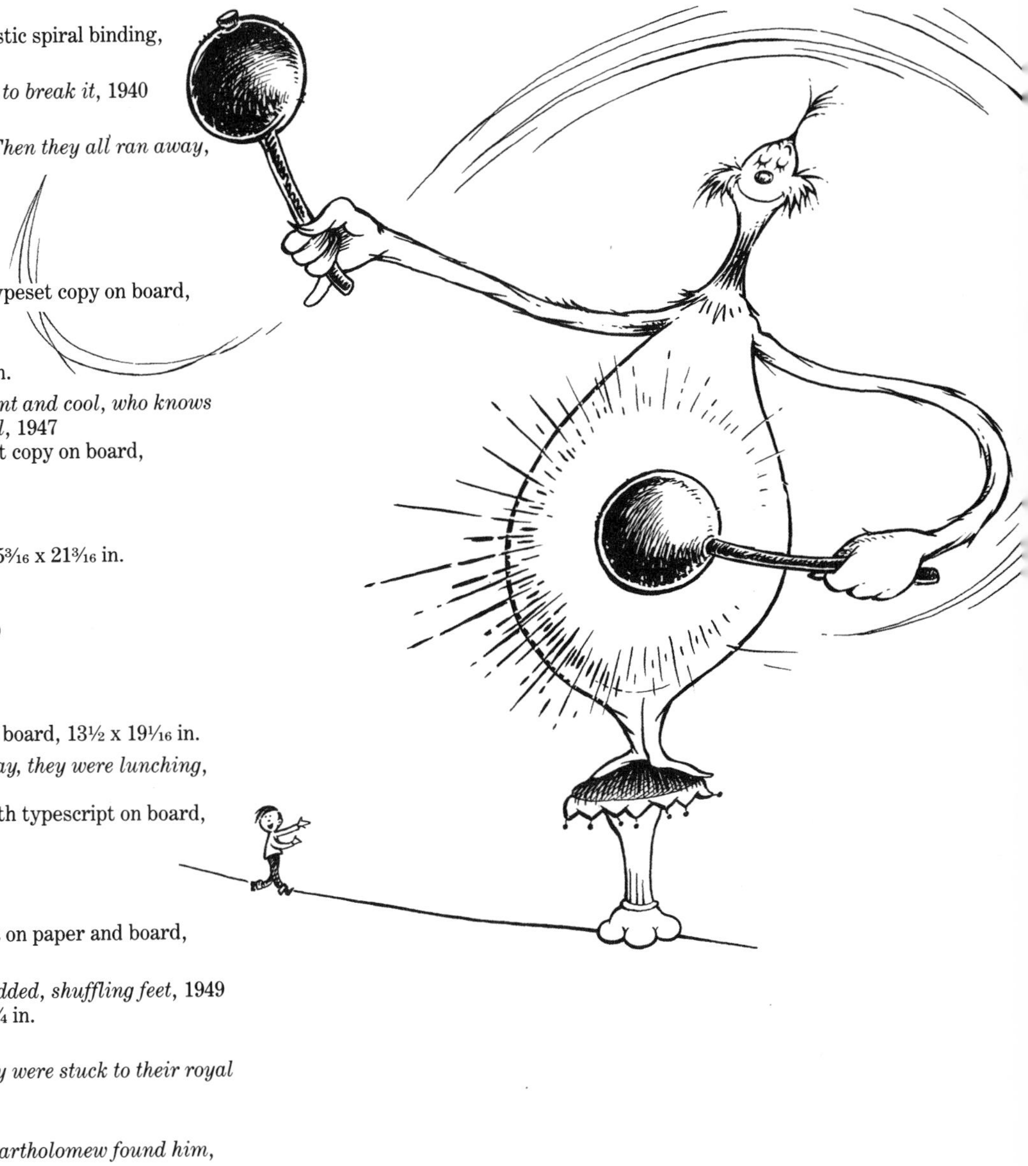

***If I Ran the Zoo* (1950)**

- 106. Presentation copy, 1950
  12¼ x 9¼ in.
- 107. *I'll go and I'll hunt in my Skeegle-mobile*, 1950
  pencil, pen, and watercolor on board, 19 x 15 3/16 in.
- 108. *I'll bring back an Obsk*, 1950
  pencil and ink on board, 18¾ x 13⅞ in.
  Collection of Theodor S. Geisel

109. *And then, just to show them, I'll sail to Ka-Troo*, 1950
pencil, ink, and watercolor with typescript on board, 20 x 27¼ in.

***Scrambled Eggs Super!* (1953)**

110. *They sailed out to sea to go looking for Grice*, 1953
pencil and ink on board, 19 5/16 x 26⅞ in.

111. *I had all I needed! And now for the cooking*, 1953
pencil and ink, 19 1/16 x 27⅛ in.

***Horton Hears a Who!* (1954)**

- 112. Presentation copy, 1954
  11¼ x 8 5/16 in.
- 113. *"Mr. Mayor! Mr. Mayor!" Horton called*, 1954
  pencil and ink, 17 5/16 x 23 3/16 in.

***On Beyond Zebra!* (1955)**

114. Working rough drawing, 1955
pencil and crayon, 13⅝ x 10¼ in.

- 115. *Most people are scared to go on and beyond*, 1955
  pencil and ink with typescript, 14½ x 21½ in.

***If I Ran the Circus* (1956)**

116. Presentation copy, 1956
11¼ x 8 5/16 in.

117. Mock-up of dust jacket, 1956
pencil, watercolor, and crayon, 11 9/16 x 24⅜ in.

- 118. Dedication page, 1956
  pencil, watercolor, and crayon, 11 x 8 in.

119. *I think I will call it the Circus McGurkus*, 1956
pencil and ink with typescript and tissue and acetate overlays, 14½ x 21¼ in.

120. *And on Stage Number Two*, 1956
pencil and ink with typescript and tissue and acetate overlays, 14½ x 21 1/16 in.

121. *And now* Here! *In this cage is a beast most ferocious*, 1956
pencil and ink with typescript and tissue and acetate overlays, 14½ x 21 1/16 in.

***How the Grinch Stole Christmas!* (1957)**

- 122. Presentation copy, 1957
  11¼ x 8¼ in.

123. Cover, 1957
pencil, watercolor, and crayon, 16¼ x 14⅝ in.

124. *Then the Whos, young and old, would sit down to a feast*, 1957
pencil and crayon with typescript, 11⅝ x 18¾ in.

- 125. *Then he slid down the chimney*, 1957
  pencil and ink with typescript, 15 1/16 x 21 in.

126. *But the sound wasn't sad!*, 1957
pencil and crayon with typescript, 11½ x 18½ in.

***The Cat in the Hat* (1957)**

- 127. *We looked! Then we saw him step in on the mat!*, 1957
  pencil and crayon with typescript, 8⅝ x 11 in.
- 128. *We looked! Then we saw him step in on the mat!*, 1957
  pencil, ink, and crayon with typescript and tissue overlay, 16 1/16 x 22 1/16 in.

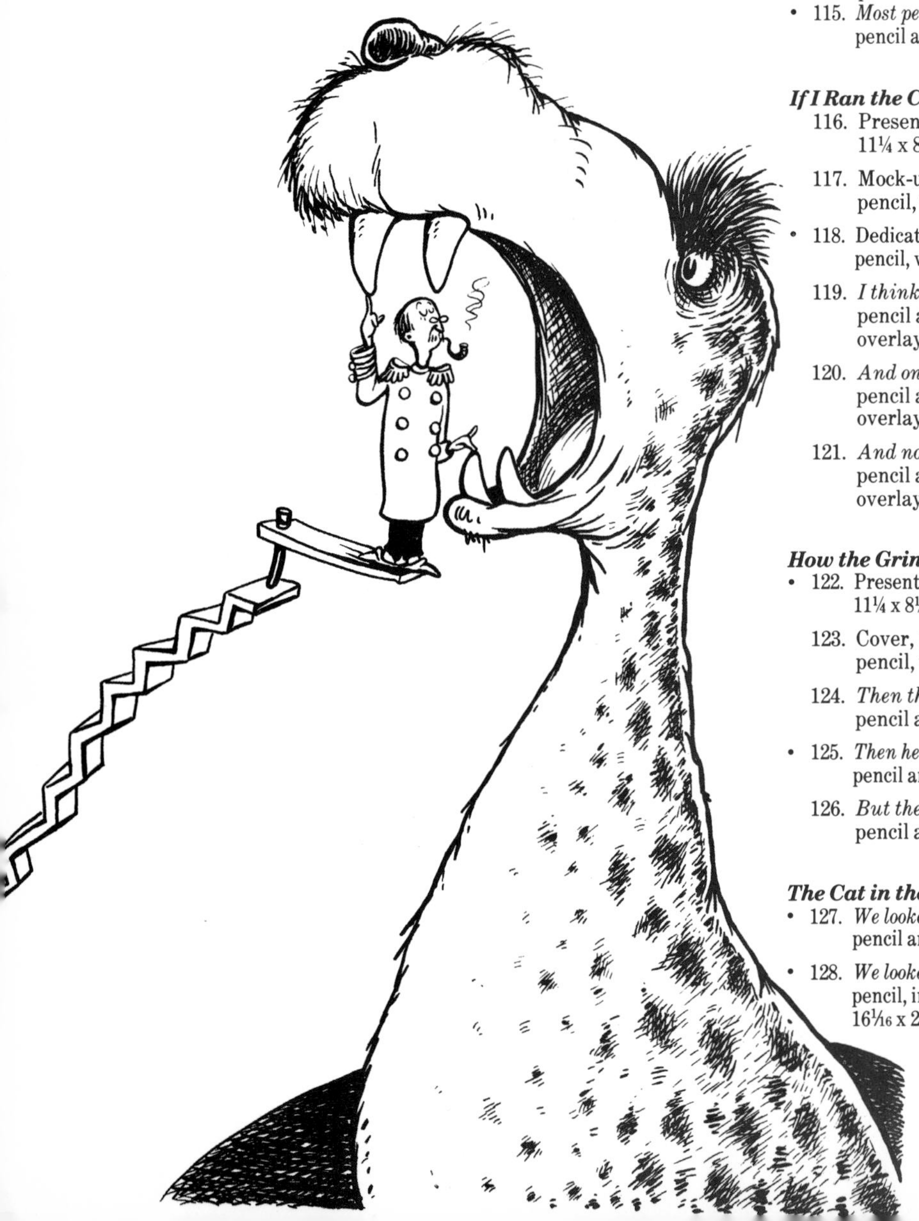

129\. *"I know some good games we could play," said the cat*, 1957
pencil, ink, and crayon with typescript and tissue overlay, 16 1/8 x 22 1/16 in.

130\. *But our fish said, NO NO! Make that cat go away!*, 1957
pencil, ink, and crayon with typescript on board and tissue overlay, 16 x 22 in.

131\. *Look at me! Look at me!*, 1957
pencil and ink with typescript and tissue overlay, 13 1/2 x 22 1/16 in.

• 132. *Now look what you did!*, 1957
pencil, ink, and crayon with typescript and tissue overlay, 16 1/8 x 22 1/16 in.

• 133. *Then out of the box came Thing Two and Thing One!*, 1957
pencil and ink with typescript and tissue overlay, 16 1/16 x 22 1/16 in.

• 134. *And then he was gone with a tip of his hat*, 1957
pencil and ink with typescript and tissue overlay, 13 7/8 x 22 1/16 in.

The Cat in the Hat Comes Back **(1958)**

• 135. Braille edition, transcribed by Evelyn Paulson, Brooklyn Industrial Institute for the Blind, 1965
felt, cotton, plastic spiral binding, 11 1/16 x 10 in.

• 136. *He was eating a cake in the tub!*, 1958
pencil and ink on board, 13 7/8 x 19 in.

137\. *The way I take spots off a dress is just so!*, 1958
pencil, ink, and watercolor with typeset copy, 11 1/16 x 15 11/16 in.

• 138. *The three of us! Little Cats B, C and A!*, 1958
pencil, ink, and watercolor with typeset copy, 12 1/16 x 16 1/2 in.

Yertle the Turtle and Other Stories **(1958)**

139\. *And all through that morning*, 1958
ink and crayon with typeset copy, 13 15/16 x 19 9/16 in.

• 140. *"You hush up your mouth!,"* 1958
pencil, ink, and crayon with typeset copy, 13 15/16 x 19 9/16 in.

Happy Birthday to You! **(1959)**

• 141. Presentation copy, 1959
11 x 8 3/8 in.

142\. Endpapers, 1959
pencil, ink, and watercolor on board, 19 9/16 x 25 1/8 in.
Collection of Theodor S. Geisel

143\. *And so, as the sunset burns red in the west*, 1959
pencil, ink, and watercolor on board, 14 15/16 x 21 7/8 in.

144\. *Now this Birthday Pal-alace, as soon you will see*, 1959
pencil, ink, and watercolor on board, 15 3/4 x 21 3/4 in.

• 145. *Look! Dr. Derring's Singing Herrings!*, 1959
pencil, ink, and watercolor on board, 14 15/16 x 22 in.

146\. *Now, by Horseback and Bird-back and Hiffer-back, too*, 1959
pencil, ink, and watercolor on board, 14 15/16 x 21 15/16 in.

• 147. *So that's what the Birthday Bird does in Katroo*, 1959
pencil, ink, and watercolor on board, 15 15/16 x 22 1/16 in.

One Fish Two Fish Red Fish Blue Fish **(1960)**

148\. Endpapers, 1960
pencil and ink on board with tissue overlay, 15 x 20 in.

149\. *Yes. Some are red. And some are blue*, 1960
pencil, ink, and typescript on board with tissue overlay, 15 x 20 in.

Green Eggs and Ham **(1960)**

• 150. Cover, 1960
pencil, ink, and watercolor with acetate overlay, 17 x 14 in.

151\. *Sam I Am*, working rough drawing, 1960
pencil, crayon, and cut paper, 8 1/2 x 11 in.

152\. *Sam I Am*, 1960
pencil, ink, and crayon on board with tissue overlay, 15 x 20 in.

153\. *I do not like them, Sam-I-Am*, 1960
pencil, ink, and crayon on board with tissue overlay, 15 x 20 1/8 in.

154\. *Would you like them here or there?*, 1960
pencil, ink, and crayon on board with tissue overlay, 15 x 20 in.

155\. *Would you eat them in a box?*, 1960
pencil, ink, and crayon on board with tissue paper, 15 x 20 in.

156\. *Sam! If you will let me be*, 1960
pencil, ink, and crayon on board with tissue overlay, 15 x 20 1/16 in.

157\. Untitled, 1960
pencil, ink, and crayon on board with tissue overlay, 15 x 20 1/16 in.

158\. *Say! I like green eggs and ham!*, 1960
pencil, ink, and crayon on board with tissue overlay, 15 1/16 x 20 1/16 in.

The Sneetches and Other Stories **(1961)**

159\. *"Belly stars are no longer in style," said McBean*, 1961
pencil and ink on board with typescript and tissue overlay, 15 x 20 1/8 in.

160\. *And Then They Moved! Those empty pants!* from "What Was I Scared of?," 1961
pencil and ink on board, 15 x 20 in.
Collection of Theodor S. Geisel

Dr. Seuss's Sleep Book **(1962)**

• 161. Cover, 1962
pencil, ink, and crayon, 11 1/4 x 10 11/16 in.

• 162. *The Hinkle-Horn Honking Club just went to bed*, 1962
pencil, ink, and crayon, 13 1/4 x 17 1/2 in.

• 163. *The Collapsible Frink just collapsed in a heap*, 1962
pencil, ink, and crayon, 13 7/8 x 17 1/2 in.

164\. *A Chippendale Mupp has just bitten his tail*, 1962
pencil, ink, and crayon, 13 3/4 x 17 3/4 in.

165\. *The Bumble-Tub Club is now dreaming afloat*, 1962
pencil and ink on board, 15 x 20 in.
Collection of Theodor S. Geisel

• 166. *Ninety-nine zillion nine trillion and two creatures are sleeping!*, 1962
pencil, ink, and crayon, 13 5/16 x 17 3/4 in.

Dr. Seuss's ABC **(1963)**

• 167. *Big R little r Rosy Robbin Ross*, 1963
pencil, ink, and crayon with typeset copy and tissue overlay, 10 x 14 15/16 in.

• 168. *I am a Zizzer Zazzer Zuzz*, 1963
pencil, ink, and crayon with typeset copy and tissue overlay, 10 x 14 15/16 in.

Hop on Pop **(1963)**

169\. *Red Red they call me Red*, 1963
pencil, ink, and crayon with typeset copy on board with tissue overlay, 10 1/8 x 15 1/16 in.

170\. *HOP POP we like to hop*, 1963
pencil and ink with typeset copy on board with tissue overlay, 10 x 15 1/8 in.

Fox in Socks **(1965)**

171\. *Sue sews socks of fox in socks now*, 1965
pencil and ink with typeset copy on board with tissue overlay, 10 x 15 in.

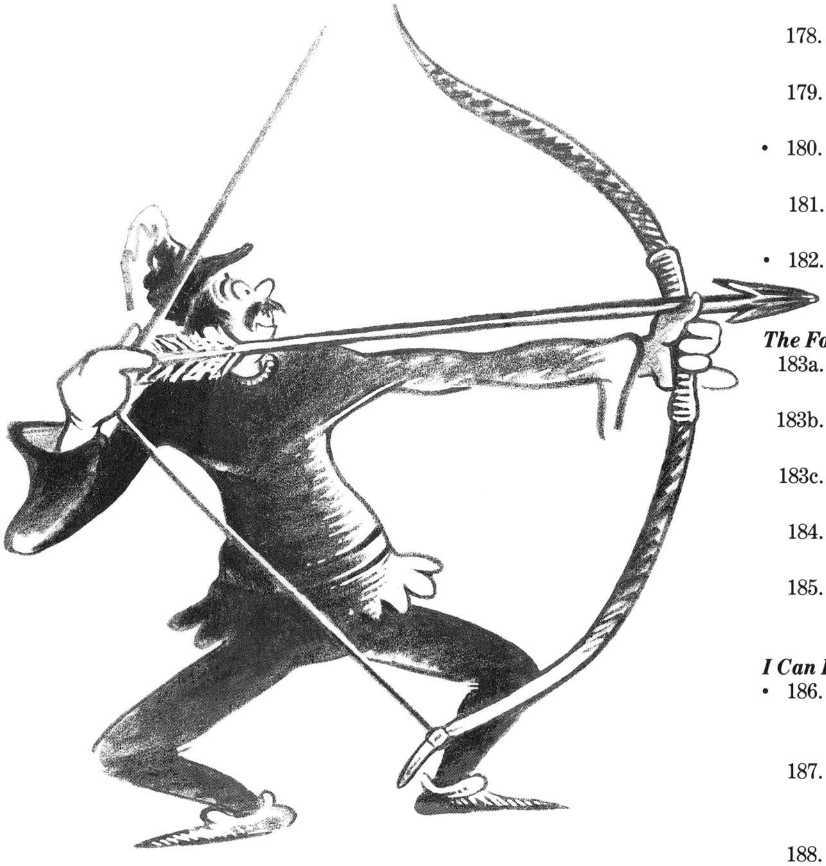

172. *Luke Luck likes lakes*, 1965
pencil and ink with typeset copy on board with tissue overlay, 10 1/16 x 15 in.

***I Had Trouble in Getting to Solla Sollew* (1965)**

173. *I jumped up behind him*, 1965
pencil and ink on board, 14 3/8 x 19 7/8 in.

174. Endpapers, 1965
pencil and ink on board, 14 3/4 x 20 1/16 in.

***The Cat in the Hat Song Book* (1967)**

175. Preliminary drawing for cover, 1967
crayon, 11 1/4 x 8 1/4 in.

176. *Yawn Song*, 1967
pencil, ink, and crayon, 14 1/8 x 18 1/16 in.

• 177. *Yawn Song*, 1967
pencil and ink with photocopy mock-up, 14 5/8 x 22 in.

178. Endpapers, 1967
pencil and crayon, 11 5/8 x 17 1/8 in.

179. Endpapers, 1967
pencil and ink with tissue overlay, 14 1/2 x 22 in.

• 180. Preliminary drawing, 1967
pencil and crayon with photocopy mock-up, 11 x 15 7/16 in.

181. Preliminary drawing, 1967
pencil and crayon, 11 1/4 x 16 1/2 in.

• 182. Three preliminary drawings for song, 1967
pencil and crayon, 11 x 8 1/2 in. each

***The Foot Book* (1968)**

183a. *Front feet... back feet*, 1968
pencil and crayon, 8 3/4 x 6 3/4 in.

183b. *Front feet back feet*, 1968
pencil and crayon, 8 3/4 x 13 15/16 in.

183c. *Front feet back feet*, 1968
pencil and ink, 14 1/4 x 19 1/2 in.

184. *His feet her feet*, 1968
pencil, ink, and crayon with typeset copy, 11 1/8 x 14 1/4 in.

185. *Up in the air feet*, 1968
pencil, ink, and crayon with typeset copy, 11 x 14 1/16 in.

***I Can Lick 30 Tigers Today! and Other Stories* (1969)**

• 186. *I can lick twenty-two tigers today*, 1969
ink and watercolor on board, 15 x 20 1/16 in.
Collection of Theodor S. Geisel

187. *Well, all was fine in Katzen-stein* from "King Looie Katz," 1969
ink and watercolor on board, 15 1/16 x 20 1/8 in.
Collection of Theodor S. Geisel

188. *The last cat in line* from "King Looie Katz," 1969
ink and watercolor on board, 15 1/16 x 20 1/16 in.
Collection of Theodor S. Geisel

189. *He simply yelled, "I QUIT!"* from "King Looie Katz," 1969
ink and watercolor on board, 15 x 20 in.
Collection of Theodor S. Geisel

190. *Then Prooie Katz slammed Blooie's tail* from "King Looie Katz," 1969
ink and watercolor on board, 15 x 20 1/16 in.
Collection of Theodor S. Geisel

191. *And that is how I found them* from "The Glunk That Got Thunk," 1969
ink and watercolor on board, 15 x 20 in.
Collection of Theodor S. Geisel

***Mr. Brown Can Moo! Can You?* (1970)**

192. Rough drawing for title page, 1970
pencil and ink, 12 1/16 x 9 1/16 in.
Collection of Theodor S. Geisel

193a. *He can go like the rain*, 1970
pencil and crayon, 10⅛ x 14⅜ in.
Collection of Theodor S. Geisel

193b. *He can go like a clock*, 1970
pencil and crayon with holograph copy, 10⅛ x 14½ in.
Collection of Theodor S. Geisel

193c. *Mr. Brown is smart!*, 1970
pencil and crayon, 10⅛ x 14⅜ in.
Collection of Theodor S. Geisel

***The Lorax* (1971)**

• 194. Preliminary drawing for cover, 1971
pencil and crayon, 11¼ x 8¼ in.
Collection of Lyndon Baines Johnson Library and Museum, Austin, Texas

195. *The Street of the Lifted Lorax*, 1971
pencil and crayon, 11 x 8⅛ in.
Collection of Lyndon Baines Johnson Library and Museum, Austin, Texas

196. *Way back in the days when the grass was still green*, 1971
pen and ink on board, 14½ x 18½ in.
Collection of Lyndon Baines Johnson Library and Museum, Austin, Texas

197. *The instant I'd finished, I heard a* ga-Zump!, 1971
pencil and crayon, 11½ x 16⅝ in.
Collection of Lyndon Baines Johnson Library and Museum, Austin, Texas

198. *And, in no time at all*, 1971
pen and ink on board, 14⁹⁄₁₆ x 18⅝ in.
Collection of Lyndon Baines Johnson Library and Museum, Austin, Texas

199. *You're glumping the pond where the Humming Fish hummed!*, 1971
pencil and crayon, 11⁵⁄₁₆ x 16⅜ in.
Collection of Lyndon Baines Johnson Library and Museum, Austin, Texas

200. *And at that very moment, we heard a loud whack!*, 1971
pen and ink on board, 14½ x 18⅞ in.
Collection of Lyndon Baines Johnson Library and Museum, Austin, Texas

201. *"SO . . . Catch!" calls the Once-ler*, 1971
pen and ink on board, 14½ x 19⅛ in.
Collection of Lyndon Baines Johnson Library and Museum, Austin, Texas

***Marvin K. Mooney Will You Please Go Now!* (1972)**

202. Cover, 1972
pencil and ink with tissue overlay, 13⅝ x 10⅞ in.
Collection of Theodor S. Geisel

203. Endpapers, 1972
pencil and ink with typeset copy, 11½ x 15¾ in.
Collection of Theodor S. Geisel

204a. Final drawings, 1972
pencil and ink with typeset copy, approx. 11¾ x 15⅝ in. each
Collection of Theodor S. Geisel

204b. Final drawings, 1972
pencil and ink with typeset copy, approx. 11¾ x 15⅝ in. each
Collection of Theodor S. Geisel

204c. Final drawings, 1972
pencil and ink with typeset copy, approx. 11¾ x 15⅝ in. each
Collection of Theodor S. Geisel

***Did I Ever Tell You How Lucky You Are?* (1973)**

205. *Just suppose, for example, you lived in Ga-Zayt*, 1973
pencil and ink, 13⅝ x 18⁹⁄₁₆ in.
Collection of Theodor S. Geisel

• 206. *Just suppose, for example, you lived in Ga-Zayt*, 1973
crayon on photostat, 12¹⁄₁₆ x 17 in.
Collection of Theodor S. Geisel

207. *And while we are at it, consider the Schlottz*, 1973
pencil and ink, 13¾ x 18⅝ in.
Collection of Theodor S. Geisel

208. *And poor Mr. Potter, T-crosser, I-dotter*, 1973
pencil and ink, 13⁹⁄₁₆ x 18½ in.
Collection of Theodor S. Geisel

***The Shape of Me and Other Stuff* (1973)**

209. Preliminary drawing for cover, 1973
pencil and crayon, 10½ x 7½ in.
Collection of Theodor S. Geisel

210. Cover, 1973
pencil and ink, 11½ x 14⅝ in.
Collection of Theodor S. Geisel

211a. Endpapers, 1973
pencil and ink, 11½ x 14½ in.
Collection of Theodor S. Geisel

211b. *And the shape of camels*, 1973
pencil and ink, 11⁹⁄₁₆ x 14⁷⁄₁₆ in.
Collection of Theodor S. Geisel

211c. *And the shapes of spider webs and clothes!*, 1973
pencil and ink, 11¹¹⁄₁₆ x 14½ in.
Collection of Theodor S. Geisel

211d. *Suppose you were shaped like these*, 1973
pencil and ink, 11½ x 14½ in.
Collection of Theodor S. Geisel

***There's a Wocket in My Pocket!* (1974)**

212. Cover, 1974
pencil and ink, 14⅝ x 11½ in.
Collection of Theodor S. Geisel

213. Endpapers, 1974
pencil and crayon, 11 x 13¹⁵⁄₁₆ in.
Collection of Theodor S. Geisel

214. Preliminary drawing, 1974
pencil and crayon, 10¼ x 14 in.
Collection of Theodor S. Geisel

215. *The only one I'm really scared of is that VUG under the RUG*, 1974
pencil and crayon, 10⅞ x 14 in.
Collection of Theodor S. Geisel

216. *Like the TELLAR*, 1974
pencil and crayon, 11½ x 14½ in.
Collection of Theodor S. Geisel

217. *And the Geeling on the ceiling*, 1974
pencil and crayon, 11 x 13¹⁵⁄₁₆ in.
Collection of Theodor S. Geisel

***Oh, the Thinks You Can Think!* (1975)**

• 218. *You can think about red*, 1975
pencil and crayon, 11⅜ x 16⅜ in.
Collection of Theodor S. Geisel

219. *And sometimes think about Bloof*, 1975
pencil and crayon, 11¹¹⁄₁₆ x 16⅜ in.
Collection of Theodor S. Geisel

***The Cat's Quizzer* (1976)**

• 220. Cover, 1976
pencil and crayon on photostat with tissue overlay, 13⅛ x 9¼ in.
Collection of Theodor S. Geisel

221. *Now look at this*, 1976
pencil and crayon, 11 x 16 in.
Collection of Theodor S. Geisel

222. *Quiz about the page before*, 1976
pencil and crayon, 11 x 16 in.
Collection of Theodor S. Geisel

223. *Here are Four What?*, 1976
pencil and crayon, 10⅞ x 15⅞ in.
Collection of Theodor S. Geisel

I Can Read with My Eyes Shut! **(1978)**

• 224. Preliminary drawing for cover, 1978
pencil, ink, and crayon, 11 x 8½ in.
Collection of Theodor S. Geisel

• 225. *If you read with your eyes shut*, 1978
crayon on photostat with acetate and tissue overlays,
13¹⁵⁄₁₆ x 17¼ in.
Collection of Theodor S. Geisel

Oh Say Can You Say? **(1979)**

226. Color proof, 1979
9 x 6½ in.
Collection of Theodor S. Geisel

227. Working rough drawing, 1979
pencil and crayon, 10¼ x 14³⁄₁₆ in.
Collection of Theodor S. Geisel

228. *If you like to eat potato chips*, 1979
pencil and ink with acetate and tissue overlays,
12⅞ x 17⅜ in.
Collection of Theodor S. Geisel

• 229. *Upon an island hard to reach*, 1979
pencil and ink with acetate and tissue overlays,
13³⁄₁₆ x 17½ in.
Collection of Theodor S. Geisel

Hunches in Bunches **(1982)**

230. Endpapers, 1982
pencil and ink, 11⅝ x 16½ in.
Collection of Theodor S. Geisel

231. Two color proofs for endpapers, 1982
10⅜ x 7½ in.
Collection of Theodor S. Geisel

232. *Then a Spookish Hunch suggested*, 1982
pencil and ink, 11⁹⁄₁₆ x 16⅛ in.
Collection of Theodor S. Geisel

233. *Way up top I met a DOWN Hunch*, 1982
pencil and ink, 11¾ x 16¼ in.
Collection of Theodor S. Geisel

234. *Then things got really out of hand*, 1982
pencil and ink with typeset copy, 11⅝ x 16⅛ in.
Collection of Theodor S. Geisel

The Butter Battle Book **(1984)**

235. *With my Triple-Sling-Jigger*, 1984
pencil and crayon, 11 x 14 in.
Collection of Theodor S. Geisel

236a. *Well...we didn't* do, *sir*, 1984
pencil and crayon, 11¼ x 16½ in.
Collection of Theodor S. Geisel

236b. *Well...we didn't* do, *sir*, 1984
pencil and ink, 13¹⁄₁₆ x 17⅞ in.
Collection of Theodor S. Geisel

236c. *Well...we didn't* do, *sir*, 1984
photo negative, 12 x 18 in.
Collection of Theodor S. Geisel

• 237. *Those Boys in the Back Room Sure Knew How to Putter!*, 1984
pencil and crayon, 11 x 16⅝ in.
Collection of Theodor S. Geisel

Memorabilia

- 238. *It all starts with Dr. Seuss*, 1955
button, 4 in. diam.
Collection of Theodor S. Geisel

239. *Reading... it all starts with Dr. Seuss*, 1978
bookmark, 2¼ x 8 in.
Collection of Theodor S. Geisel

240. Dr. Seuss Flag, c. 1975
nylon, fabric appliqué with metal grommets, 60 x 192 in.
Collection of Theodor S. Geisel

Book in Progress

***You're Only Old Once!* (1986)**

241. Bone Pile, 1986
pencil, ink, and crayon, approx. 8½ x 11 in. each
Collection of Theodor S. Geisel

242a. Manuscript (stage 2), 1986
typescript with holograph corrections, 11 x 8½ in.
Collection of Theodor S. Geisel

242b. Manuscript (semifinal stage), 1986
typescript with holograph corrections, 11 x 8½ in.
Collection of Theodor S. Geisel

242c. Manuscript (edited final text), 1986
typescript with holograph corrections, 11 x 8½ in.
Collection of Theodor S. Geisel

- 243a. Working rough drawings, 1986
pencil, ink, and crayon with holograph copy,
approx. 11⅝ x 16⅝ in. each
Collection of Theodor S. Geisel

243b. Working rough drawings, 1986
pencil, ink, and crayon with holograph copy,
approx. 11⅝ x 16⅝ in. each
Collection of Theodor S. Geisel

243c. Working rough drawings, 1986
pencil, ink, and crayon with holograph copy,
approx. 11⅝ x 16⅝ in. each
Collection of Theodor S. Geisel

243d. Working rough drawings, 1986
pencil, ink, and crayon with holograph copy,
approx. 11⅝ x 16⅝ in. each
Collection of Theodor S. Geisel

243e. Working rough drawings, 1986
pencil, ink, and crayon with holograph copy,
approx. 11⅝ x 16⅝ in. each
Collection of Theodor S. Geisel

243f. Working rough drawings, 1986
pencil, ink, and crayon with holograph copy,
approx. 11⅝ x 16⅝ in. each
Collection of Theodor S. Geisel

244. Four finished drawings, 1986
pencil and ink, approx. 14½ x 18⅛ in. each
Collection of Theodor S. Geisel

245. Four hand-colored photostats, 1986
ink and crayon on photostat, 13 x 18 in. each
Collection of Theodor S. Geisel

246. Color chart, 1985
22 x 28 in.
Collection of Theodor S. Geisel

247. Progressive proofs, 1986
25⅝ x 37½ in. each
Collection of Theodor S. Geisel

248. Book-binding paper and color samples, 1986
various sizes
Collection of Theodor S. Geisel

249a. Trial binding, 1986
11⅜ x 8¾ in.
Collection of Theodor S. Geisel

249b. Trial binding, 1986
11⅜ x 8¾ in.
Collection of Theodor S. Geisel

249c. Trial binding, 1986
11⅜ x 8¾ in.
Collection of Theodor S. Geisel

250. Final binding, 1986
11⅜ x 8¾ in.
Collection of Theodor S. Geisel

251. Dust-jacket color proofs, 1986
11¼ x 24¼ each
Collection of Theodor S. Geisel

252. Production copy, 1986
11¼ x 8⅜ in.
Collection of Theodor S. Geisel

Bibliography

Books by Dr. Seuss

And to Think That I Saw It on Mulberry Street. New York: Vanguard Press, 1937.

The 500 Hats of Bartholomew Cubbins. New York: Vanguard Press, 1938.

The King's Stilts. New York: Random House, 1939.

The Seven Lady Godivas. New York: Random House, 1939.

Horton Hatches the Egg. New York: Random House, 1940.

McElligot's Pool. New York: Random House, 1947. Caldecott Honor Book.

Thidwick the Big-Hearted Moose. New York: Random House, 1948.

Bartholomew and the Oobleck. New York: Random House, 1949. Caldecott Honor Book.

If I Ran the Zoo. New York: Random House, 1950. Caldecott Honor Book.

Scrambled Eggs Super! New York: Random House, 1953.

Horton Hears a Who! New York: Random House, 1954.

On Beyond Zebra! New York: Random House, 1955.

If I Ran the Circus. New York: Random House, 1956.

How the Grinch Stole Christmas! New York: Random House, 1957.

The Cat in the Hat. New York: Beginner Books, Random House, 1957.

The Cat in the Hat Comes Back. New York: Beginner Books, Random House, 1958.

Yertle the Turtle and Other Stories. New York: Random House, 1958.

Happy Birthday to You! New York: Random House, 1959.

One Fish Two Fish Red Fish Blue Fish. New York: Beginner Books, Random House, 1960.

Green Eggs and Ham. New York: Beginner Books, Random House, 1960.

The Sneetches and Other Stories. New York: Random House, 1961.

Dr. Seuss's Sleep Book. New York: Random House, 1962.

Dr. Seuss's ABC. New York: Beginner Books, Random House, 1963.

Hop on Pop. New York: Beginner Books, Random House, 1963.

Fox in Socks. New York: Beginner Books, Random House, 1965.

I Had Trouble in Getting to Solla Sollew. New York: Random House, 1965.

The Cat in the Hat Song Book. New York: Random House, 1967.

The Foot Book. New York: Bright & Early Books, Random House, 1968.

I Can Lick 30 Tigers Today! and Other Stories. New York: Random House, 1969.

I Can Draw It Myself. New York: Beginner Books, Random House, 1970.

Mr. Brown Can Moo! Can You? New York: Bright & Early Books, Random House, 1970.

The Lorax. New York: Random House, 1971. National Council for the Social Studies Notable Children's Trade Book/Social Studies.

Marvin K. Mooney Will You Please Go Now! New York: Bright & Early Books, Random House, 1972.

Did I Ever Tell You How Lucky You Are? New York: Random House, 1973.

The Shape of Me and Other Stuff. New York: Bright & Early Books, Random House, 1973.

There's a Wocket in My Pocket! New York: Bright & Early Books, Random House, 1974.

Oh, the Thinks You Can Think! New York: Beginner Books, Random House, 1975.

The Cat's Quizzer. New York: Beginner Books, Random House, 1976.

I Can Read with My Eyes Shut! New York: Beginner Books, Random House, 1978.

Oh Say Can You Say? New York: Beginner Books, Random House, 1979.

Hunches in Bunches. New York: Random House, 1982.

The Butter Battle Book. New York: Random House, 1984.

You're Only Old Once! New York: Random House, 1986.

Collaborations

Ten Apples Up on Top. Written by Theo Le Sieg (pseud.) and illustrated by Roy McKie. New York: Beginner Books, Random House, 1961.

The Cat in the Hat Dictionary. Illustrated by P. D. Eastman. New York: Random House, 1964.

I Wish That I Had Duck Feet. Written by Theo Le Sieg (pseud.) and illustrated by B. Tobey. New York: Beginner Books, Random House, 1965.

The Eye Book. By Theo Le Sieg (pseud.). New York: Bright & Early Books, Random House, 1968.

My Book about Me. By Dr. Seuss and Roy McKie. New York: Beginner Books, Random House, 1969.

Great Day for Up! Written by Dr. Seuss and illustrated by Quentin Blake. New York: Bright & Early Books, Random House, 1974.

OTHER SOURCES

Selected Articles

Bandler, Michael J. "Dr. Seuss: Still a Drawing Card." *American Way,* December 1977, 23-27.

Bunzel, Peter. "Wacky World of Dr. Seuss." *Life,* 6 April 1959, 107-9.

Cahn, Robert. "The Wonderful World of Dr. Seuss." *Saturday Evening Post,* 6 July 1957, 17-19, 42-46.

Corwin, Miles. "Author Isn't Just a Cat in the Hat." *Los Angeles Times,* 27 November 1983, 1, 3.

Crichton, Jennifer. "Dr. Seuss Turns Eighty." *Publishers Weekly,* 10 February 1984, 22-23.

Curley, Suzanne. "The Nuclear Dr. Seuss." *Newsday,* 5 March 1984, 3.

Dow, Maureen. "Novel 'Ironweed' and Mamet Play Are Awarded 1984 Pulitzer Prizes." *New York Times,* 17 April 1984, A1, B4.

Geisel, Theodor. "If at First You Don't Succeed—Quit!" *Saturday Evening Post,* 28 November 1964, 8-9.

Gorney, Cynthia. "Dr. Seuss." *Washington Post,* 21 May 1979, B1, B3.

Hacker, Kathy. "Happy Eightieth Birthday, Dr. Seuss." *Philadelphia Inquirer,* 7 March 1984, E1, E8.

Kahn, Jr., E. J. "Profile: 'Children's Friend.' " *New Yorker,* 17 December 1960, 47-93.

Katz, Lee Michael. "Most Kids Say Yooks Should Talk to Zooks." *USA Today,* 29 June 1984, A11.

Kupferberg, Herbert. "A Seussian Celebration." *Parade,* 26 February 1984, 4-6.

Lyon, Jeff. "Writing for Adults, It Seems, Is One of Dr. Seuss' Dreams." *Chicago Tribune,* 15 April 1982, 3:1, 10.

Sullivan, John. "Growing up with Dr. Seuss." *American Baby,* August 1984, 46, 52.

Wilder, Rob. "Catching up with Dr. Seuss." *Parents Magazine,* June 1979, 60-64.

Books

Bader, Barbara. *American Picturebooks from Noah's Ark to the Beast Within.* New York: Macmillan Publishing Co. Inc., 1976.

Blackbeard, Bill, and Martin Williams, eds. *The Smithsonian Collection of Newspaper Comics.* Foreword by John Canaday. Washington, D.C., and New York: Smithsonian Institution Press and Harry N. Abrams, Inc., 1977.

Cianciolo, Patricia. *Illustrations in Children's Books.* Dubuque, Iowa: Wm. C. Brown Co., 1970.

Cott, Jonathan. *Pipers at the Gates of Dawn: The Wisdom of Children's Literature.* New York: Random House, 1981.

Fisher, Margery. *Who's Who in Children's Books: A Treasury of the Familiar Characters of Childhood.* New York: Holt, Rinehart and Winston, 1975.

Lukens, Rebecca J. *A Critical Handbook of Children's Literature.* 2d ed. Oxford, Ohio: Miami University, 1982.

MacCann, Donnarae, and Olga Richard. *The Child's First Books: A Critical Study of Pictures and Texts.* New York: H. W. Wilson Co., 1973.

Meigs, Cornelia, et al. *A Critical History of Children's Literature.* Rev. ed. New York: Macmillan Co., 1969.

WEST BEAST
EAST BEAST

Photography Credits

All black-and-white illustrations are by Library Photographic Services, University of California, Los Angeles, unless otherwise noted. All color illustrations are by Michael Arthur.

Nancy Crampton, p. 80; Alan Decker, p. 80; Jill Krementz, p. 79.

Dr. Seuss from Then to Now
was originally published in 1986 by
The San Diego Museum of Art
Edited by Kathleen Preciado and Letitia O'Connor
Designed by Dana Levy, Perpetua Press, Los Angeles
Typeset by Continental Typographers, Chatsworth, California
First Random House Edition 1987